PRIVATE EYE ANNUAL 2018

EDITED BY IAN HISLOP

Published in Great Britain by
Private Eye Productions Ltd
6 Carlisle Street, London W1D 3BN

www.private-eye.co.uk

© 2018 Pressdram Ltd
ISBN 978-1-901784-66-4
Designed by Bridget Tisdall
Printed and bound in Italy
by L.E.G.O. S.p.A

2 4 6 8 10 9 7 5 3 1

PRIVATE EYE ANNUAL 2018

EDITED BY IAN HISLOP

"Not for me, I've got work in the morning"

Royal Mail bows to pressure and releases set of stamps to commemorate Brexit

To reflect the national mood, the Royal Mail is proud to present a set of two Brexit designs. These will be issued in books of 100 stamps, containing 52 stamps for Leavers and 48 stamps for Remainers.

Price £1 or €1

THE BIBLICAL TIMES

FRIDAY 6 OCTOBER 2017

JC personality cult queried

by St Matthew Parris

OKAY he's the Messiah, but does everyone have to be quite so grovelling? The quiet seaside town of Galilee has been overtaken by a hoard of 12 fanatics who worship every word he says and think he walks on water, which incidentally he wants to nationalise, or turn into wine, depending on whom you believe.

I'm not saying that some of his points aren't quite interesting, such as promoting "a gentler, kinder form of world in which neighbours love each other", and I can see the attraction of all those glib slogans like "blessed are the peacemakers", "the meek shall inherit the earth" and "forgive Diane, she knows not what she is doing". But the reality of the man they call Jezza C is that he's just an ordinary bloke with a beard and sandals who doesn't like to wear a tie, but who seems to have captured the popular imagination.

But is he really "The Saviour", or is he just an opportunist? And what about the people around him? Many of them are zealots and determined tax collectors. And where are the women? Will this bunch of disciples turn into a force for good if they are allowed to take over and run things? Or will they become intolerant and start smiting non-believers?

The moment they all started singing the football chant "*O, Come All Ye Faithful!*" was when I started to have my doubts. This much adulation just can't be good for him. I see trouble ahead. And what about his attitude to the Jews? (*continued Chapter 94*)

OLIVIA COLMAN TO BECOME QUEEN

by Our Showbiz Staff **Phillipa Page**

HER Majesty the Queen has decided to stand down and is to be replaced by the popular actress Olivia Colman.

The star of *Peep Show* and *Broadchurch* has agreed to take over the role in 2019 and has already begun rehearsals.

Some commentators were surprised that the normal protocols were not observed and that the more traditional heirs to the Crown were overlooked.

Said a palace spokesman, "The Royal Family decided not just to skip a generation but to skip everyone in line for the job and to give it instead to Olivia.

"The reasons are fairly obvious," he continued. "We thought that, in the modern context, it had to be a woman and we wanted to choose someone that the public loves."

Critics have complained that Olivia Colman already has all the public roles that are going and that it is not fair for her to be given the Queen too.

"She's in everything," said one. "Why has she got to be in the most expensive drama series in the world as well?"

But, on the whole, the news has been welcomed across the country and even the Archbishop of Canterbury has expressed his delight. He told reporters, "There is no one more suitable to be Monarch and Head of the Broadchurch of England".

LOCKER ROOM ETIQUETTE
A PRESIDENT'S GUIDE

'Taking a knee'

Deeply unpatriotic and offensive gesture committed by loser athletes during the national anthem, protesting about so-called police killings of black people. Never happened. Fake news! Blame on both sides! Get over it! I blame crooked Hillary! Lock her up! And the athletes. The sons of bitches should be fired! Have you seen the NFL ratings? #Sad!

'Grabbing a pussy'

Deeply patriotic and inoffensive gesture committed by winning millionaire/TV star/politician during national campaigning, protesting against women refusing to sleep with him on account of his so-called stupid hair and small hands. Never happened. Fake news! Blame on one side! Get over it! I blame crooked Hillary! Lock her up! And the women! The bitches should be fired! Have you seen my rantings? #Not sad!

BORIS GOES JOGGING WITH SUN EDITOR

Nice tits!

SUN READERS' LETTER OF THE WEEK

■ Given that Boris seems to go jogging all the time – why doesn't it have any effect?
Ena B. Weightwatcher

The Eye's Controversial New Columnist

The columnist who has personally gnawed all the EU safety marks off his plastic bricks

This week I am very angry that no babies are being called "Nigel" anymore. Speaking as a baby (*see photo*), I think this is a great shame. Surely we can't let this glorious name go the way of "Adolf" and "Genghis"? To this end, I have done my bit and called all my cuddly toys Nigel. This has instantly transformed my life. Nigel the happy-looking teddy has urged me to leave the house, break all ties to the stifling bureaucracy of my mum and dad and strike out for a new parental deal with the oddly-shaped gnome in the garden. Nigel the teddy also proposes a rally to highlight this sad state of affairs where everyone wears black shirts in mourning for the death of the name "Nigel" and I, for one, see no problem with (*cont. p94*)

"I suppose a lot of people do their worshipping online these days"

Pound now worth nothing

THE Royal Mint warned members of the public that as of last weekend, their pound coins were worth absolutely nothing.

Consumers will no longer be able to use the old round pound to buy goods or services, nor will they be able to use the nice shiny new one, nor the two pound one, the plastic five pound note, the tenner with Jane Austen on it, the twenty or, well, let's face it, any of it.

Said a spokesman, "The pound is weakening by the minute, particularly against the Zimbabwean billion-dollar note, and we are advising shops to start trading in an alternative currency, such as shells, glass beads, beans, or better still, the Euro."

He continued, "The collapse in the value of the pound is entirely due to fear of Brexit / fear of Corbyn's spending policies / fear of Hammond's spending policies / fear of fear itself. Please delete according to political preference."

ON OTHER PAGES: 'Poundland' to be renamed 'Land'.

DePress Association

Tesht Match Shpecial
Live from Drunk-as-Lords

Aggers: And you join us after tea... well, after dinner, actually... it's two in the morning here at the Mbargo nightclub.

Boycott: So Ben Stokes and Alex Hales have been in for some time now...

Aggers: Not the most reliable partnership.

Boycott: No, but once Stokes had dodged that bouncer, you knew he was going to stick around for the long haul.

Aggers: Oh and Stokes is going for a quick single, and another, and another...

Boycott: Aye, the lad's unstoppable when he's in this kind of mood. It's help yourself time!

Aggers: Stokes is on 37 – he's going to beat Botham's average of over 40 in a night.

Boycott: Now it's the drinks interval – time to take a break from the drinking to do some fighting.

Aggers: We should see some fireworks. You have to say, Ben Stokes is surely the country's best all-rounder – a fantastic boozer and an accomplished hitter.

Boycott: Amazingly quick hands!

Aggers: Oh no! Stokes has been caught! Caught on CCTV!

Boycott: The video review is pretty clear. And he's out. Of the test side. What a silly boy.

Andrew (*aka* Statters): This the first time that a batsman has been caught and dropped at the same time!

Boycott: Oh dear. And now it's the long walk for Stokes – all the way to court number 14.

(continued 94 kHz)

R.I.P. HUGH HEFFNER

First time he's been stiff in ages

Playboy man not dead

THE WHOLE world was in mourning last night at the news that the man most famous for appearing on the cover of Playboy had not died.

The millionaire playboy, Donald Trump, was known for his sleazy womanising and for hanging around with models far younger than himself, and, in some cases, marrying them.

A keen golfer, he was rarely photographed without a buggy (surely "bunny"?) at his side. But sources confirm last night that Donald Trump is still alive and well and threatening to kill everyone else. *(Rotters)*

THIS WEEK

ITV's AMANDA HOLDEN interviews Astronaut TIM PEAKE

Have you got a favourite moon?

Well, I think you...

Have moons played a significant role in your career?

No, I actually trained for a rather different...

Moon-wise, do you think that the Moon has been important to you?

I have never been to the Moon. I was on the space station. No one has been to the Moon since 1972.

(Long pause)

Has anything amusing ever happened to you in connection with the Moon?

Only this interview.

NEXT WEEK: *Ben Shephard, "Me and My Shepherd"*

GRASSROOTS SHOCK

We've got to appeal to young Tories

We ARE the young Tories

"Just be myself? Fine, I'll go cry in the shower"

HOLLYWOOD DISOWNS SHAMED WEINSTEIN

The only job I'll get now is being President

You'll never w**k in this town again

AN APOLOGY
on behalf of two former Presidents of the USA
(and their First Ladies)

IN COMMON with each other, and indeed the entire Hollywood movie industry, we may in recent years have given the impression that we thought that Mr Harvey Weinstein, the well-known film producer, was in some way a major force for good in American culture and society. When we fêted Mr Weinstein at White House events, welcoming him with affectionate hugs and posing for photographs with him, as we told everyone present "Harvey is the most wonderful human being in the world", "Harvey is a genius and a legend" and "Harvey is God", we may have led our fellow Americans to believe that we in some way held Mr Weinstein in the highest esteem.

We now realise, in the light of recent revelations, that Mr Weinstein is in fact one of the most disgusting and loathsome sex offenders that the world has ever known, who has done more to drag the good name of Hollywood into the slime of moral degradation than anyone in its long and distinguished history. What we should obviously have said to this repulsive serial sex pest, when he had the audacity to turn up at 1600 Pennsylvania Avenue, was "Mr Weinstein, it's good of you to give that enormous cheque to the Democratic funds, but just leave it in the hall and go out the back through the kitchen".

We, the Clintons and the Obamas, are very pleased to issue this clarification and would like to say how deeply sorry we are for ourselves that we've been caught out fawning over this unspeakable monster who somehow managed to hide his true nature from no one except ourselves.

A postscript to the above apology from President Clinton

MAY I say that I myself am particularly shocked by the idea of a man in a position of great power attempting to coerce a young woman into granting him sexual favours in return for a promise that he might advance her career. In all my life I have never come across anything so deeply upsetting and Hillary wishes me to say that she agrees with every word of this statement.

Exclusive to all newspapers

WHY, OH WHY, DIDN'T I SAY ANYTHING EARLIER?

THE silence has been deafening. For years I have sat typing up promotional guff for all the films Harvey told me were marvellous, without ever mentioning the sordid truth about his treatment of young actresses.

How could I do it? That is the question facing me today, but instead I'm going to write a piece attacking everyone in Hollywood for keeping quiet as the movie mogul monster was allowed to rampage unchecked.

Shame on everyone, apart from me! The Luvvies, the Producers, the Publicists, the Actresses themselves – all of them guilty of a complicit and deadly silence, which I knew about but thought I probably wouldn't mention, in case I didn't get invited to his Oscar night party.

GREAT SCENES FROM THE MOVIES

Jabba The Harvey

HOLLYWOOD IN SHOCK
by Our Showbiz Correspondent

THERE was disbelief right across Hollywood today after it was revealed that legendary producer Harvey Weinstein had used his position of power to take advantage of young women.

"This has blown my mind, do men in Hollywood really do that?" said Roman Polanski.

"The level of disrespect he has for women, treating them as commodities for his sexual gratification is jaw dropping," said Charlie Sheen.

"I am shocked to my core that a man could behave in a sexually repulsive way to a young woman," added Woody Allen.

"He has shamed us as a community," added an ashen-faced Bill Cosby.

"Sex pests have no place in Hollywood," added former Fox News host Bill O'Reilly.

All men in Hollywood agreed that such behaviour would never be tolerated in Hollywood.

Try not to take all the weight on your head.

MOZ

THE WEINSTEIN SCANDAL
FLEET STREET ROUND-UP

Daily Mail

Weinstein was hypocritical monster who exploited women and shamed his industry.

Inside: 94-page special featuring all the half-naked actresses as you've never seen them before! Plus all the juicy titillating details of their horrific and deeply upsetting experiences on the casting couch.

The Sun

SWEINSTEIN! This sleazy media mogul should be ashamed of himself for encouraging innocent girls to strip off in order to further their careers.

Said one, curvy Katie, 19: "Everyone knew that Rupert was only interested in one thing – money."

The Daily Telegraph

My afternoon alone with the King of Sleaze – nothing happened!

Allison Pearson tells all (about her film and book, *I don't know how she gets away with it*, but tells us very little about Mr Weinstein).

DAILY EXPRESS

Did Weinstein ever try it on with Diana?
Page 2: No

TODAY PROGRAMME CENSURED FOR ALLOWING ELDERLY MAN TO TALK NONSENSE WITHOUT BEING CHALLENGED

That Transcript In Full

(Pips...)

Nick Robinson: You're listening to *Today*. And here are the headlines again... The *Today* programme has been rebuked by the BBC complaints unit, which found that the programme allowed noted climate-change sceptic Lord Lawson to repeat a lot of factual inaccuracies that went unchecked.

Sarah Montague: It's claimed that the *Today* programme, in its never-ending and ultimately futile quest to balance both sides of every single issue, no matter how ridiculous, ended up sounding completely biased and a wee bit bonkers.

Nick Robinson: So that's what *they* say... In the interests of presenting the other side of that issue, we have someone on the line who says that the *Today* programme is doing a fabulous job – Lord Lawson.

Lord Lawson: Delighted to be here, Nick.

Nick Robinson: So, the *Today* programme. You think they're doing really well?

Lord Lawson: Oh, indeed. I have statistics that show the *Today* programme is better than it's ever been and also that climate change is a fantasy invented by the EU to distract from their secret takeover by giant lizards pretending to be Angela Merkel and Jean-Claude Juncker.

Nick Robinson: Thank you, Lord Lawson.

THOSE NEW ROYAL MAIL STAR WARS STAMPS IN FULL

Jeremy Corbyn
WRITES

HELLO! It's me again. I would like to take this opportunity to thank all of you out there for sending me such great questions to read out at Prime Minister's question time.

There have been so many highlights, but particular thanks to Mrs Gladys Cartwright from Penge, whose letter about nice young policemen failing to turn up at her house when she rings to complain about her neighbour slamming his car door at 9 o'clock at night was a real zinger and certainly had the PM squirming!

All in all, my idea of addressing real people's concerns via the pulpit of PMQs has been an unquestioned triumph and a real way of putting democracy back in the hands of you, the Great British Public!

But amidst all this back slapping, a tiny minor grumble and a bit of a plea from me. You have been sending me a lot of questions about Brexit. Now, I hardly need to remind you, the Great British Public, that the Great British Public are hardly interested in this subject. They want their questions answered about the NHS and railways and things like that. You know, stuff that I like to talk about all the other times.

Here, for example, is a typical letter from Mr Bob Sponge from Wolverhampton. He writes: "Dear Jeremy, I am very worried about the chronic underfunding of the NHS under the Tories…", which is a jolly promising start! But then he goes on "…which I'm concerned would only get worse if our trade deficit goes belly up and we'll have no tax receipts because of Brexit." You see, it all starts to lose its way after the word "Tories" and my eyes start glazing over.

So, here's a tip. If you want to get your letter on the telly, give me a question about homelessness and NHS waiting times and Ken Loach and Trade Unions and things like that. Things that the Great British Corbyn are interested in. A question about Brexit? Sorry! Boring!

Now I'm not telling you what to write, but I just don't want you wasting your money on a stamp! Especially now that it swells the coffers of the hated Post Office shareholders! Cheerio!

BEING HAPPY IN YOUR OWN SKIN IS ALL ABOUT FEELING TOTALLY AT EASE WITH YOURSELF...

AND HAVING A CLEAR UNDERSTANDING OF WHO YOU REALLY ARE AND WHAT MAKES YOU FEEL FULFILLED...

YEAH, TOTALLY.

DEBS, WOULD YOU SAY THAT YOU'RE HAPPY IN YOUR SKIN...?

I WOULD, GARY, YES.

SINCE ALL THE NIPS AND TUCKS, I'M VERY HAPPY THANK YOU.

IT FITS YOU LIKE A GLOVE AGAIN, BABES...

JOHNSON, DEBS AND I HAVE SIX GUESTS FOR DINNER THIS SATURDAY... WE'D LIKE YOU TO COOK SOMETHING SPECIAL...

VERY GOOD, SIR.

ANY VEGETARIANS, VEGANS OR PESCATARIANS?

NO.

ANY SPECIAL DIETARY REQUIREMENTS, FOOD ALLERGIES OR GLUTEN INTOLERANCE...?

NONE.

HOW PECULIAR... THAT'S WHAT WE THOUGHT. THEY ARE A BIT OF A WEIRD BUNCH.

HAS SIR HAD A CREATIVE TEMPER TANTRUM?

RECORDING STUDIO

SOMEONE IN THE BAND SAID SOMETHING AND I GOT ANGRY...

WHAT A MESS...

COME ON. IT'S NOT THE FIRST TIME I'VE BROKEN STUFF: HOTEL ROOMS, STUDIOS, GUITARS, MARRIAGES...

I'M DESTRUCTIVE... I'VE BROKEN PRETTY MUCH EVERYTHING THERE IS TO BREAK IN MY LIFE...

NONSENSE, SIR...

YOU NEVER BROKE AMERICA, DID YOU?

RECORDING STUDIO

DON'T YOU START. THAT'S WHAT SET ME OFF...

LIKE SIMON COWELL, I'VE GIVEN UP USING MY MOBILE PHONE... I HAVEN'T USED IT FOR MONTHS...

JUST LIKE SIMON I'VE FOUND GIVING UP MY MOBILE HAS MADE ME HAPPIER... IT'S EMPOWERING...

AND LIKE HIM I'VE BECOME WAY MORE FOCUSED AND AWARE OF THE PEOPLE AROUND ME...

MY P.A., DIARY SECRETARY, P.R... THEY MAKE AND TAKE ALL MY CALLS FOR ME...

GARY BLOKE'S PHONE...

DEBS, I AM NOT INSENSITIVE AND EMOTIONALLY IMMATURE WHEN IT COMES TO WOMEN, AS YOU ALLEGE.

FAR FROM IT. I MAY BE A ROCK STAR BUT I'M AN OLD SCHOOL ROMANTIC TRADITIONALIST AT HEART.

I'M REALLY SENSITIVE AND CAN GET EMOTIONAL VERY EASILY...

I CRIED AT ALL OF MY WEDDINGS, DIDN'T I, JOHNSON?

ER...YES, SIR...

HEIR OF SORROWS
A Short Story Special
by Dame Sylvie Krin, author of *Duchess of Hearts* & *You're Never Too Old*

THE STORY SO FAR: Charles and Camilla are attending the naming ceremony of the new aircraft carrier HMS Prince of Wales. Now read on...

THE wind whipped across the old naval dockyard at Rossnoble in Forsytheshire, as the Royal party were escorted to the dais erected in front of the awesome three-billion-tonne colossus of the seas.

The band of the 17th Royal Bank of Scotlanders struck up with a jaunty rendition of "*All the nice girls love a sailor*" as Camilla mounted the platform, with Charles dressed in the full ceremonial uniform of the Vice Ruler of the Queen's Navy – with medals for distinguished service in the Gilbert & Sullivan Islands.

The suave figure of Rear Admiral Insurance-Smythe pointed to the grey leviathan sitting in the dock.

"When it's finished, sire, it'll have 360° multi-role global air-sea functionality with all- theatre operational capability."

"Excellent," Charles replied enthusiastically, though privately experiencing a small pang of regret that his namesake ship had been made out of drab modern steel rather than, say, traditional British oak, and that its design, to be honest, more resembled an NCP car park than the glorious bemasted sailing titans of yore: *The Mary Archer... The*

Golden Globe... The Cutty Budget...

His reverie was interrupted by the silky-tongued master mariner, "...and here, Ma'am, is the whisky..." The Admiral then handed Camilla a bottle of the finest 81-year-old Glen Campbell.

"Cheers!" she replied heartily. "I'm absolutely gasping for a snifter."

"It's not for drinking, old sausage," Charles chided. "It's for launching the ship. You smash it on the poop-stern." He struggled to remember the correct nautical terminology from his days as midshipman on *HMS Appalling*.

"What a waste!" sighed the Duchess of Cornwall, as she reluctantly hurled the exquisite double-peaty malt at the ship's side.

"I name this ship... HMS Charley McCharlesface... only kidding, Chazza...!"

Charles looked unamused. "...*HMS Prince of William*... no, that can't be right... hang on... *HMS Prince of Wales*! That's it!"

The band struck up the theme tune from the Captain Birdseye advertisement and a group of jolly jack tars in hi-vis bell-bottoms danced a traditional hornpipe whilst throwing their hard hats in the air.

Charles felt a surge of pride. This grand, majestic vessel was, in its way, a symbol of his own imminent launch into the high seas of public life – modern, dignified and powerful, yet still embodying the proud heritage of Britannia's rule over the waves. Yes, it was high time that the Prince of Wales began his epic voyage into the briny future...

UNFORTUNATELY, at that precise moment, the wind swooping down from the slopes of Ben Preston carried the unkind words of the bearded Captain Pugwash, the veteran of many a fierce battle in the corridors of Whitehall, who was standing on the ship's forward Ant deck...

"Bloody waste of money. We've got *The Queen Elizabeth* at sea already. *The Prince of Wales* is out of date before it's even launched. It's too late. Might as well keep it in dry dock or, better still, scrap the tub altogether and move on to a new generation that is more suitable to the modern era..."

The band, meanwhile, had segued into the solemn strains of the hymn "*Abide with me*". Charles's spirits sank, like the unfortunate *SS Titanic*, into the depths of Davy Davies's locker, as the gulls cried mournfully overhead...

(To be continued...)

PRIVATE SHEEP'S EYE
— Friday, 6 October 2017 —

WORLD REJOICES AT LIBERAL SAUDI MOVE

THERE was widespread delight as Saudi's conservative rulers lifted a centuries-old ban on women driving.

The authorities have declared that women may now drive lorries into crowds, and suicide trucks packed with explosives – but not in Saudi, obviously. As the world's leading exporters of terrorism, it was only going to be a matter of time before they embraced the new world and encouraged women to take their rightful place behind the atrocities that we see. (*You're fired. Ed.*)

Moderate Saudi Arabia to emerge

SAUDI Arabia's crown prince, Mohammed Dusty bin Salman, has vowed to transform the kingdom and turn it into a new "moderate" country.

"From now on, we're all about being moderate – there will only be moderate stoning to death of non-believers, only moderate torture of political prisoners and only moderate repression of all dissent and especially moderate carpet bombing of civilians in Yemen," bin Salman told the Guardian.

"And, from next year, instead of being banned from driving, women will be free to be taught a lesson. By which, I mean they will be beaten moderately by their moderate husbands in the comfort of their own homes.

"This will transform our image, so that governments like Britain no longer face embarrassing questions about selling us immoderate amounts of arms." (*Rotters*)

Uber to go to Appeal Court

by Our Transport Staff
Ivor Satnav

THE head of the online taxi firm Uber has today announced that he will be challenging Transport for London's decision to remove Uber's licence in the courts.

Said the firm's boss, Iranian-American businessman Mr Beardy Khashkhow, "We are going straight to the Appeal Court. Just as soon as I can find out where it is. Do you know? I only got here this morning. Is it near Harrods? Hang on, give me the postcode and..."

Mr Khashkhow went on to explain that, despite having previously refused to improve standards at Uber, TfL's decision to ban him had changed his mind.

"I am now going to do an unexpected U-turn," he said, "like most of my drivers when they consult the satnav."

Mr Khashkhow concluded, "TfL's decision is grossly unfair and I am appealing."

"No, you're not," replied nearly everybody.

Rodin's Wishful Thinker

NEW UKIP LOGO UNVEILED

Go back to Africa!

YES! IT'S PESTMINSTER

What's this about misconduct?

I have never met Miss Conduct! Her allegations are all false

HAD AN ACCIDENT AT WORK?
SLIP, TUMBLE or FALL?

✔ Have you FALLEN short of the usual high standards expected of a parliamentarian?

✔ Has your hand ACCIDENTALLY FALLEN on an aide's knee?

✔ Did you TUMBLE OVER on to the floor and mistakenly look up someone's skirt?

✔ Have you SLIPPED and ACCIDENTALLY lunged at someone with your lips pursed?

✔ Whilst making a small point of order with your thumb & forefinger, did you ACCIDENTALLY TRIP and pinch the bottom of your PA?

✔ Did you SLIP UP and erroneously text a picture of your genitals to your researcher?

WESTMINSTER SEX TOYS

BIG BEN — BLACK ROD

THE HONOURABLE MEMBER

TORY

ROBERT THOMPSON

It's absolutely disgusting that the other side have grotesque misogynist pervs amongst them, explain both parties

A SPOKESMAN for the Labour/Conservative party issued a statement this morning, saying that the disgusting sex-pest behaviour exhibited by Mr Jared O'Mara/Mr Stephen Grabb was a sign that the Labour/Conservative party had a serious and uncontrollable problem with sexual abuse which was definitely limited to their party and no other.

"Yet again, we see the other side have a splinter in their eye," the spokesmen continued, not visibly distressed by the plank in their own. "Until they get their house in order, we are the only party fit to govern Britain."

© *Wandering Hansard 2017.*

THAT KINNOCK APOLOGY HE HASN'T MADE YET IN FULL

I would like to totally and utterly and utterly totally apologise for Michael Gove's sexist, misogynist and misogynistically sexist joke on the Today programme about Harvey Weinstein, which was inappropriate, not appropriate and entirely without any appropriateness, and in response to which I immediately expressed my total and utter disgust by laughing and making a joke of my own, making a parallel between John Humphrys' interviewing technique and Weinstein's groping, which was in no way and entirely not in any way similar, the same, or bearing any similitude to Gove's totally utterly unacceptable joke which was entirely typical of the outdated, out-of-date, and date outed Tory approach to women, which *(cont. p994)*

Construction 'Placed On Hold'
by Our Political Staff **Alan Wicca**

IN THE wake of the suicide of Welsh Labour AM Carl Sargeant, construction of a giant Wicker Man to dispense summary justice for any public official accused of sexual harassment has been temporarily halted.

"We're now thinking that instead of immediately hurling anyone accused of being a vile pervert into the Wicker Man, we'll see that the accusations are thoroughly investigated and the claims tested in a court of law and only then will these individuals' good names be rightfully destroyed," said a baying Twitter mob.

"Relying on due process and the rule of law to establish guilt rather than marching the accused straight to the Wicker Man may seem controversial in this social media age, but we're willing to give it a try."

NAVY FAILED TO CONTROL COCAINE ABUSE

I see no shit

Carry On Up Periscope!

Hilarious new film captures Britain's modern Navy at its finest

Starring: *Sid James as Captain Hornyblower, Kenneth Williams as Rear-Admiral Rear, Barbara Windsor as Chief Pretty Officer Rumpy-Pumpy, and Charles Hawtrey as Able-Seaman Seaman*

SCENE: On board HMS Insatiable, the men and women of the state-of-the-art XXX class nuclear submarine have been at sea for almost 15 minutes.

HORNYBLOWER: I'm dying for it – my country that is!

RUMPY-PUMPY: Ooh! Cheeky! Is that a Trident missile or are you just pleased to see me?

HORNYBLOWER: Well, it certainly goes off with a big bang!

ADMIRAL REAR: What's up?

HORNYBLOWER: Nothing yet... give us a second!

RUMPY-PUMPY: Ooh-er! *(dirty giggle)*

ADMIRAL REAR: Dive! Dive! Dive!

HORNYBLOWER: Well, if that's an order, sir!

(HORNYBLOWER and RUMPY-PUMPY disappear from view)

SFX: Toiiiiinnnggg!

(A bra lands in Rear-Admiral Rear's face)

ADMIRAL REAR: What depth are we?

(HORNYBLOWER comes into view briefly)

HORNYBLOWER: We've hit the bottom, sir!

RUMPY-PUMPY: Ooh! Saucy!

ADMIRAL REAR: I knew having women on board was a mistake!

HORNYBLOWER: I'm having all the women on board I can! *(dirty laugh)*

(Enter SEAMAN SEAMAN to make dramatic announcement)

SEAMAN SEAMAN: Incoming nukes from North Korea!

ADMIRAL REAR: We're all fucked!

HORNYBLOWER AND RUMPY-PUMPY: Saucy!

(Audience die laughing or just die, thanks to slight lack of concentration by Britain's essential first line of defence)

CLARE BALDING

Interview conducted by ~~Ginny Dougary~~ Clare's publicist, who asks proper questions and not these ridiculous so-called "journalistic" ones.

Ms Balding, ~~do you have many spoons?~~ you're looking absolutely marvellous. Do you have many spoons?

Yes, I do – I've always been a really keen spoon collector.

~~Do you have a favourite spoon?~~ That's a very funny, charming and sparkling reply. Do you have a favourite spoon?

I have – a beautiful Louis Quinze spoon with gold trefoil I was lucky enough to find at a car boot sale in Stroud.

~~This is a slightly tricky question, but do you think spoons can be overrated?~~ What's the best spoon?

Ooh, that's a hard one, but I'd have to say it's probably the good old-fashioned pudding spoon. Obviously, though, I like all spoons!

~~As a gay woman, do you think that you are a role model?~~ As a national treasure, can you tell us about your new children's book, A Spoon For Charlie?

Thank you, that's a much better question. It's all about a girl called Charlie and a racehorse called "Brilliant Broadcaster" who gets given a spoon full of sugar and they all learn some valuable life lessons.

~~Do you think it's ever appropriate for celebrities to insert plugs for their own books into interviews?~~ As your publicist, is there anything more I can ask you about spoons?

No, I think that covers everything, except to add that my book is published by Puffing Books and is available for a very reasonable £16.99.

NEXT WEEK: Another celebrity interview you can't believe a word of.

From The Message Boards

Members of the online community respond to the major issues of the day...

Ooh la la guys! Paris has its first ever nude restaurant, and vive la différence, because I can't see it catching on here. Given it's called O'Naturel, I don't imagine the Irish will be too happy either. So in these days of inappropriate advances, keep your hand on your ha'penny! – **Bogbrush**

Bogbrush, your tone is highly inappropriate, but I attribute it to ignorance rather than malice. As a Reader in Sexual Cultures, I am hoping to visit this restaurant with Cambridge academic Victoria Bateman, who challenges the association between the female body and sex, and attended a faculty meeting nude with 'Brexit leaves Britain naked' written on her breasts. I expect an altogether more mature response from the French. – **Dr Sarah Reeves**

Couldn't agree more, Sarah. I weigh 34 stone, sweat profusely, and cannot reach my genitals, anus or feet when washing. I say this without self-judgement. I am constantly frustrated by the restrictions of clothing and so-called 'normal' seating. The thought of luxuriating in an empathetic environment, while the heavenly scent of the cuisine mingles with my own natural fermentation, strikes me as a quintessentially Parisian marriage of the sophisticated and the primal. – **Madam George**

Yawn. Welcome to the bien pensant world of 'those cold and timid souls': the safe suburban 'thrill seeker', the worthy 'nudist', and the craven consensual gawper. How different, to paraphrase dear Teddy further, from the Doer of Deeds: the brazen exhibitionist, baring all under the banner 'Épater la bourgeoisie!'; and her counterpoint, the true voyeurs – that daring band of brothers who perch in precarious 'hides', illicitly install hidden cameras, and risk their liberty to covertly enjoy womankind in her most exalted state: bare and unaware. – **Monkey see**

My husband and I are in our sixties and have many hobbies, including real ale, non-league football, swinging and dogging. My dress code is always 'as little as possible'! We used to frequent the first balti houses in Birmingham, where it was normal for the boys to take their shirts off on hot nights after a few pints. One fat lad had bigger tits than me, and I told him so. Prove it, he said, and I did! Everyone cheered and the manager brought me a complimentary bottle of sweet wine for doubling the clientele. The fun continued in the car park when the restaurant closed, and we did a few more topless nights for charity until the council stepped in. – **Gilfy Gracie**

pic's or it never happened 😊 – **hatfield gooner**

They were the days before phone cameras, but the old man said I looked like a plasterer's radio by the end of the night! – Gilfy Gracie

Great stuff guys! – **Bogbrush**

Marriage beds

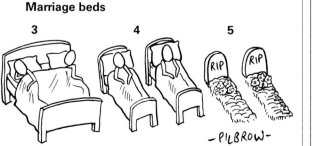

1   2   3   4   5

– PILBROW –

Boris Johnson, The Secretary of State for Foreign and Commonwealth Affairs, writes exclusively for Private Eye

CRIPES! After a bit of a hairy week, coming under fire from all and sundry, with one bound Bozza is free!

Unlike poor old Mrs Whatsherface, that journalism teacher, currently banged up in Iraq, or is it Iran? Whatever, same difference, one of those sheep-eye-munching Johnny Arab regimes which get the hump every time yours truly shoots the breeze in front of a Commons Select Committee.

I mean, there's me doing his best to use all the diplomatic lingo at my disposal, viz respectfully avoiding phrases such as towel-heads, camel-shaggers, and fornicator-floggers, when, low and behold, I'm completely stitched up like a blasphemer's mouth, by being quoted utterly in context!

For the record, I did not say that Mrs Thingummy was a spy intent on undermining the mad mullahs. On the contrary, I said she was teaching journalism, which they wantonly misinterpreted as meaning that in some way she taught journalism.

In my book, that means churning out sub-Jeeves and Woosterish nincompoopery for £250k a year, waffling away, making up long words like "blathermungus", with the odd quotation from antiquity thrown in, such as "Mea Culpa", which, as everybody

Bozza suspended! (Just kidding, Theresa wouldn't dare!)

knows, means "Don't Blame Me"!

How can anyone pretend that sort of larkish wordsmithery could possibly lead to insurrection, rebellion or the overthrow of a supposedly strong and stable Prime Minister?

Still talking about Iran, folks! Obvs! So, in summary, thanks to my esteemed and fragrant former colleague Ms Jolly Priti Patel for copping some of this week's flak for the Boz Man, and leaving me free as a bird.

Yes, the Bozmeister has once again got out of jail, and is currently working around the clock to effect similar for fellow scribe, the unfortunate Mrs Doodah. Rest assured, we'll have you out of there in five years. Ten tops. Fifteen max.

Cripes!

✡ **DAILY TELAVIVAGRAPH**

Fallout continues from secret meetings

by Our War Correspondent
Sheldon Daily

AS further details emerge of the clandestine talks between Israel and the UK, a senior member of the Government has been called in to face the music.

Benjamin Netanyahu has been asked to explain why he has become embroiled in one of the most poisonous feuds in political history, seemingly showing his hand by associating himself with Priti Patel, a hardline backer of the Brexit cause.

Brexit has been a source of bitter conflict for literally hundreds of days, tearing the area known as the "Middle England"

apart, with millions of Remainers being told they have to shift their position and relocate far away from their chosen homeland, namely Europe.

Brexiteers, on the other hand, deny it is a disaster of biblical proportions, and insist that they have a right to what they call the Promised Land, the Land of Milk and Honey, although there may be a considerable increase in the price of both milk and honey post-Brexit.

Netanyahu has been roundly condemned for getting involved in this toxic conflict which, despite several attempts at negotiation, seems no nearer to reaching a peaceful resolution.

West Bank Story

C of E to allow boys to wear dresses

by Our Religious Correspondent **Jen de Fluid**

THE Church of England has controversially decided to accept the practice of boys cross-dressing in its various establishments.

This will come as a shock to generations of parishioners who are completely unfamiliar with the sight of small boys wearing long frocks and fancy ruffs openly taking part in public church services as though this were perfectly normal.

However, a spokesman for the Church of England, wearing a long-flowing black cassock, said, "It really is

time for the Church to move into the 15th century and understand that clothing really should be non-gender-specific and that it is no big deal for boys, or indeed grown men, to abandon trousers and wear elaborate vestments, should they so desire."

Choir as folk

He added, "This shows that we are a thoroughly modern Church, not afraid to move with the times and say that we don't like women bishops... whoops, don't quote me."

HOW FAR RUSSIA HAS COME

1917	2017
■ Country run by unaccountable, super-rich elites	■ Country run by unaccountable, super-rich elites
■ Any pretence of democracy a sham	■ Any pretence of democracy a sham
■ Secret police locking people up without trial	■ Secret police locking people up without trial
■ Country engaged in grinding miserable war on its Western borders	■ Country engaged in grinding miserable war on its Western borders
■ Conditions ripe for a bloody revolution	■ Record approval ratings, leader completely untouchable

Exclusive to all newspapers

HOW COULD SEEDY PHOTOGRAPHER HAVE GOT AWAY WITH IT FOR SO LONG?*

*because you kept buying his photos

ON OTHER PAGES

● All the seedy photographer's most explicit photos for you to enjoy!

Fashion industry 'in shock'

THE fashion world was in shock today at the news that an industry which promotes nubile, semi-naked teenagers as the ideal of beauty could have a seedy side, after photographer Terry Richardson was banned from working for Condé Nast.

"We're in total shock that the fashion world is anything other than a wholesome, nurturing environment in which to take highly sexualised pictures of extremely emaciated young girls," said one fashion insider.

"I nearly sneezed out my line of coke when I heard what Terry was alleged to have got up to with his models.

"We can assure you that from now on the industry will only be employing decent, upstanding pillars of the community to take photographs of semi-naked, wide-eyed 16-year-olds, sucking suggestively on lollipops."

VOGUE
THIS SEASON'S ESSENTIALS

■ Faux-fur jackets
■ Pencil skirts
■ Keeping a straight face whilst pretending you've only just heard the allegations about Terry Richardson

Red carpet protests – the papers respond

"You applaud the actresses' feminist stance, I'll bitch about what they're wearing"

Corrections and clarifications

● In the recent series of articles published by the Guardian in collaboration with Süddeutsche Zeitung, the New York Times, the International Confederation of Investigative Journalists and various other international bodies, an unfortunate misprint occurred. The phrase "The Paradise Papers", referring to the leaked documents about off-shore tax havens, should have read "The Parasite Papers". The connotations of the word "Paradise" – palm trees, sandy beaches, golden sunshine – may well have given people the false impression that the practice of tax avoidance was in some way glamorous and aspirational, rather than seedy, greedy and anti-social. We apologise to our readers for this error repeated 788 times in every issue.

Lord Ashcroft releases results of new poll

Are my financial arrangements

A bit whiffy?	18%
Very pongy indeed?	21%
Absolutely super-smelly?	25%
Completely stinking rotten?	36%

LEWIS HAMILTON IN PRIVATE JET TAX SCANDAL

Ready for take-off, Mr Hamilton...

We'll take off 20 percent VAT for a start!

Doctors 'to ask if you're ill'

IN a move seen as highly controversial, NHS England says that, in future, GPs will be required to ask if you are ill.

"How is this going to work in practice, given we're only allowed a few minutes with each patient and most of that is taken up with asking them about their sexual orientation?" said one GP.

"I really don't see how we'll have the time to diagnose their life-threatening conditions. We're not miracle workers, you know."

NHS England insisted that any details of a patient's illness would be confidential and wouldn't be shared with third parties, such as NHS hospitals, as, let's face it, have you seen how long the waiting lists are?

But information will be shared by GP receptionists who will continue to announce loudly to the entire waiting room that you're here to see Doctor Gupta about your piles again. (Cont. p94)

WHY IS PRODUCTIVITY IN BRITAIN SO LOW?

by Our Economic Staff **Ivor Concentration-Problem**

YET again, the budget has highlighted the shameful secret at the heart of Britain's economy: that we in this country have a real problem with productivity, which remains stubbornly low compared to our international competitors.

But experts are baffled as to why, with the latest technological advances, UK output in all sectors is... hello, there's a picture of a cat that's very funny... is declining in real terms with growth impacted... #pictureofmylunch #yumyum... and remaining at levels that have not been seen since... ping! message alert: fancy a pint later?... In German industry there is no question of the importance of... Ten Celebrities Who Will Amaze You By How Fat They Are Now... and even in France, which

has traditionally been seen as a relatively unproductive... Cyber Monday Last Final Offer Deals Before Cyber Tuesday... one thing is certain, no one can yet explain just why, in offices, shops and factories all over the country, British workers are failing to keep up with their Candy Crush Level 94 Play Now... Betfair 365 Latest Odds On Next Ashes Star To Be Sent Home In Disgrace 11-2 Bet Now... Desperate Housewives in Your Area Message Now... It seems an intractable problem and, for a chancellor who is facing relentless pressures on the economy from all sides, it is perhaps the most frustratingly insoluble... If you have enjoyed this article, please give some money to the *Guardian*, please, please (*cont. 2014*)

Twitter takes to Twitter to complain about Twitter

AFTER increasing its character count to 280 words, Twitter has been attacked by many Twitter users, taking to Twitter to post on Twitter that they'll never use Twitter again.

"This has completely ruined Twitter for me," tweeted one Twitter user. "If Twitter continues in this way, I will tweet loudly and continuously about how Twitter has ruined tweeting for me. Furthermore, I will tweet about how I will soon not be tweeting until I

find something else to tweet about."

Twitter has defended itself, saying that undertaking incredibly unpopular and pointless changes that anger Twitter users is by far the most important part of Twitter.

"If we don't do this now and cause a storm of angry tweets, there'll be less to complain about when we change it back and everybody tweets about how they liked it better before."

CONSERVATIVES IN CRISIS

One day I hope to lead the Tory party

Me too!

FROM THE DAILY BREXITGRAPH

Better to be poor and free

What the Euro-bullies and our own sad Remoaners have got to realise is that when 17.5 million proud Britons voted to leave the European Union in June 2016, every single one of them knew exactly what he or she was voting for.

Any suggestion that they were not fully aware of all the implications of a vote for Leave is utterly patronising and dishonest.

What all these patriotic citizens were voting for could not have been clearer or more explicit. They wanted to leave the EU as fast as possible.

They wanted to take back control in every conceivable respect.

And they didn't want to spend a single pound more on the way out. They wanted to leave the single market and the customs union. They didn't want to obey any more of those directives and regulations with which the EU has been swamping us for decades.

And if that means we can no longer trade with Europe, so be it. If it means that we have to

stop exporting cars, chemicals, pharmaceuticals, medicines, aviation components, Welsh lamb and even cheese to our largest export market then, as the voters made clear, that is a very small price to pay for winning back our sovereignty and freedom.

Even if we have to accept the crashing to a halt of the entire UK economy, followed by the rise to power of a Soviet-style Communist command economy, where people will be lucky to find even the odd mouldy potato on the shelves of their local supermarket, that is exactly what an unarguable landslide 2 percent majority of Britain's voters were demanding.

Anyone who dares to say otherwise has not the faintest respect for democracy and is also, in failing to give their wholehearted support to Mrs May and Messrs Davis, Johnson and Fox, a traitor who deserves only to be strung up from the nearest lamp-post, or at the very least to be wished an early death from cancer by thousands of responsible and well-informed trolls on *Telegraph* online.

Philosophy – Rise and Fall

I think therefore I am...

Urrrh.. it is what it is..

17th Century   **21st Century**

THE EYE'S MOST READ STORIES

Negotiations with Britain almost complete

Theresa May said she is delighted that, 18 months after the Brexit referendum vote, there is now an end in sight to her long and, at times, fraught negotiations with Britain over the Brexit arrangements.

"I feel we are now very close to a framework that would mean that the negotiations with Britain over the type of Brexit we want are close to being completed.

"These have been long and, at times, tortuous negotiations with Britain, but I believe we have the framework of an agreement and there is a very real prospect that negotiations with Brussels over Brexit could restart on Thursday 28 March 2019."

'Millions more' now in favour of Brexit

Latest figures show that, since the 2016 referendum, several million more people are now convinced that Brexit is good news and are strongly in favour of the UK leaving the EU. These millions of new converts live mainly in Amsterdam and Paris, the new homes of the European Medicines Agency and the European Banking Authority.

"It's fabulous," said one Parisian, "new jobs, and more workers coming here to boost our economy."

Said another, "This is a smart move by the British, or I'm a Dutchman, which I am, so it's actually not smart at all."

ROYAL ENGAGEMENT

HISTORY IN THE MAKING

A prince marries an American divorcee. What can go wrong?

As long as no one dresses up as a Nazi!

PAST IS FORGOTTEN

Are there any embarrassing nude photos?

Only of you in Las Vegas!

NEW ROLE FOR ACTRESS

You can smile, you can wave – the part's yours!

I've always wanted to do Panto!

HOW THE NATION'S PRESS REACTED TO THE ROYAL WEDDING

Daily Mail

ROYAL WEDDING BREXIT BOOST SHAMES REMOANER TRAITORS

THE Sun

WATCH ALL OF MINXY MEG'S MOVIES ON SKY PREMIERE!

The Daily Telegraph

Major US-UK Alliance Signals End For EU

THE TIMES

Ms Markle's cinematographic oeuvre now available on Sky premiere

theguardian

Does mismatched couple spel end for manorchy?

DAILY EXPRESS

COLD WEATHER COULD MEAN WINTER

FINANCIAL TIMES

Markle in coalition to save career

theCanary

Will Harry and Meghan include pledging allegiance to Corbyn in their wedding vows?

What will Meghan's royal title be? You decide...

The Princess of Wales
The Duchess of Windsor
The Princess of Suits
The Duchess of Duke Street
The Duchess of Hazzard
The Marchioness of Markle
The Dowager Lady Grantham
Dame Meggie Smith
Baroness Meggie Thatcher
Baroness Rumpy-Pumpington
The Mystic of Meghan
The Countess of Monte Python
The Duchess Potato
The Duchess Original Oatmeal And Ginger Fruity Crumpet
Queen Meghan, Khaleesi of the Great Grass Sea,
Lady Regnant of the Seven Kingdoms, Breaker of Chains, Mother of Dragons

(That's enough titles. Ed)

POETRY CORNER

**In Memoriam
Antonio Carluccio, celebrity chef**

So. Farewell
Then Antonio Carluccio,
Italian chef,
Restaurateur and
Culinary legend.

They called you
"The Godfather of
Italian Cooking",
But there was no
Horse's head in
Your lasagne.

You had a way with pasta
But now, alas,
You have pasta-way.

As Nigella tweeted,
"Riposi in Pace",
Which I think I
Will make tonight,
In your memory.

E.J. Thribborini (17½ courses)

17

ASSAD AND PUTIN TALK TRADE

We're hoping to buy lots of Russian gas...

Mustard or sarin?

YOUR ECONOMIC WORRIES ANSWERED

Q: Is Britcoin a real currency and will I lose money if I hold on to it?

A: The pound, or Britcoin as it is sometimes referred to in the media, is an unstable and unpredictable currency often used by speculators in shady deals or in money laundering operations and is not advisable for use by ordinary consumers. In recent years the Britcoin has been talked up, but then it crashed spectacularly with huge losses to investors. At present, the Britcoin remains fragile and ordinary punters are advised to stick to a better regulated, more reliable currency, such as the Venezuelan Bolivar or the Zimbabwean Mugabe.

Jeremy Clarkson

The danger of Legless Drivers

I am one of the most famous drivers, not just in the country, but in THE WORLD. And take it from me, I've tried all kinds of driving in all kinds of cars: Driverless Cars, Carless Drivers, even Carless Cars.

But believe me, the most dangerous thing on the road nowadays is the Legless Driver. I've been there, done it, missed dinner, punched the producer, got fired and bought the "No one's watching Amazon" t-shirt.

What on earth gave the Powers That Be the idea that filling a finely-tuned driving machine with gallons of high-octane liquid alcohol would result in anything other than a career car crash of biblical proportions *(cont. 194mph)*

HOME DELIVERY

stokoe

How David Cassidy was my first teenage crush and wrote the soundtrack to my youth

by All Middle-Aged Female Columnists

YOU might call it "Puppy Love" *(subs, please check this is one of his)*, but to those of us growing up in the Sixties or Seventies *(subs, please check)*, lying in our bedrooms looking at the posters on the wall, there was only ever one Eva Cassidy.

Nothing could stop us watching the Alan Partridge Family on the television and imagining that we too were part of that wonderful fictional world of The Brady Bunch.

The stepson of Mama Cass and Dave Dee, he was hotter than hot pants, and as Cool as the Gang. The hair, the flares, the Fonz, they were innocent Happy Days. The death of David Cameron is a true tragedy. *(Note from subs: Are you sure this is what you mean?)*

At least we can still enjoy his music because he hasn't yet been accused of inappropriate behaviour *(subs, please check quite extensively, as he had a younger fanbase)*. And I will never get that song out of my head, when he and his brother Butch rode around on bicycles singing "Raindrops keep falling on my head".

'Security services knew all about terrorists and would definitely have stopped them if only they'd realised what the terrorists were up to' claim security services

by Our Intelligence Staff ■ ■

A SHOCK new report commissioned by Home Secretary Amber Rudd has revealed that the intelligence services were already "on the track" of several of the terrorists behind this year's unprecedented spate of terror attacks.

David Anderson QC, in his review of the background to the Manchester, London Bridge and other atrocities, finds that the perpetrators had been well known to MI5, MI6 and the police for months before the attacks took place, but unfortunately they had "failed to put two and two together in time to stop them".

The report quotes an unnamed senior security officer explaining, "It's easy with hindsight to say that we should have intervened earlier to prevent these terrorists doing what they did. But at the time, all we knew about them was that these young men wore beards, were sympathetic to the aims of IS and had made a number of visits to Syria and Libya, where they assured us they were 'simply on holiday'."

He continued, "We could see no reason to be suspicious of the intentions of these young men, just because their fathers were members of the 'Establish the Caliphate in Britain Now' movement and they spent eight hours a day looking at jihadi websites on their computers, plus several times had tea and prayers with Mr Anjem Choudary, the well-known Muslim cleric, now admittedly serving a short prison sentence for 'incitement to terrorism'."

The officer went on, "Of course, if we had guessed that all this activity might lead these young men to commit the very unfortunate crimes that they did, then we would have taken all the necessary actions to prevent these regrettable events taking place."

The officer concluded, "You have to remember that we in Britain have an outstanding record in counter-terrorism which is the envy of the world, and we have foiled every planned terrorist attack in recent years, except of course the ones we didn't."

The head of MI5 officially welcomed the report yesterday and said that insofar as the report was in any way critical of the intelligence services, he was sure that the necessary lessons would be learned, as they always have been in the past.

MUGABE SHOCK

They've stolen my land

ZIMBABWE REJOICES AT CHOICE OF MASS-MURDERER TO REPLACE THE PREVIOUS ONE

by Our Special Correspondent **Victoria Falls**

THERE was singing and dancing in the streets of Zimbabwe's capital city last night, as the country's entire 4 million-strong population celebrated the downfall of the hated dictator Robert Mugabe.

Old age pensioners and teenagers hugged each other and wept for joy as they realised they were finally free of a 37-year reign of terror, which had reduced their once prosperous country to economic ruin, ruled by a totally corrupt and murderous tyranny.

Harare, Harare, while euphoria lasts

The jubilant crowds hung garlands of flowers around the necks of gun-toting soldiers loyal to Mugabe's former right-hand man Emerson Mnangagangsta, who is widely tipped to step up as the country's new psychopathic despot.

After a unanimous vote in Zimbabwe's parliament to give

full democratic support to the military non-coup, Zimbabweans are over the moon at the prospect of a democratic change of dictator, and look forward to a new era of ruthless political repression and shameless kleptocracy.

Amazing lack of Grace

The only people in the world who did not join in the unanimous mood of happy optimism were the proprietors of a number of designer clothes shops, jewellers and Lamborghini dealers in Paris, London, New York and Beijing, who wept openly at the thought that never again could they expect to see their favourite customer, Zimbabwe's former first lady, Imelda Winnie Grace Mugabe.

Gerry Adams 'Standing Down'

by Our Sinn Fein Correspondent **Sam Tex**

GERRY ADAMS has announced he's standing down as Sinn Fein President and will not stand for re-election to the Irish Parliament, saying he is leaving his dream of a unified Ireland safely in the hands of Theresa May and David Davis.

"Even during my days in the IRA's Non-Military Peace Wing, I rarely witnessed two people as determined as May and Davis are to make a unified Ireland a reality, with their blundering

Brexit negotiations over the Irish border," Adams told delegates at the Sinn Fein Conference.

"What once seemed impossible in my lifetime, now, thanks to the sheer incompetence and hubris of the UK's Brexit negotiators, seems a raging certainty to happen in 2019.

"My job here is done."

THOSE MAJESTIC CREATURES OF BLUE PLANET II

Here are the denizens of the deep who've had the entire nation spellbound of a Sunday night with their ability to flourish and multiply in our oceans, with lifespans ranging from a few hundred to many thousands of years:

The carrier bag (native to British shores)

The six-pack beer holder

The single-use plastic bottle

POETRY CORNER

Lines on the retirement of Gerry Adams, peacemaker and statesman

So. Farewell
Then Gerry Adams,
You are retiring
After 34 years as
Head of Sinn Fein.

You always insisted
That you were not
A member of the IRA,
Which is why you
Have chosen to
Leave quietly,
Rather than going out
With a bang.

E.J. Thribb (17½)

THIS WEEK

WITH AUNT JULEY FROM HOWARDS END

Do you have a favourite spoon?
Yes, it's the one I spread the jam with.

But that's historically inaccurate, isn't it?
Not at all, the BBC researches these things very carefully and...

Amateur spoonologists don't agree with you. Many of them have written into *Me and My Spoon*, pointing out that Edwardian society was very hierarchical and class-based with regards to spoon/jam etiquette...
I'm not sure that is really very important in the grand scheme of things...

It is if you are a spoon. That is surely one of the themes of Forster's novel – that the cultured and idealistic Schlegels were attempting to break down cutlery-based social barriers in order to redefine Edwardian society spoonwise...
Look, it's just a costume drama on a Sunday. They didn't have television cameras in those days either.

Has anything amusing ever happened to you in connection with a spoon?
This is E.M. Forster we're talking about. You could try "Room With a Spoon"...

NEXT WEEK: *Virgina Woolf, "Me and My Wolf"*.

"Next left, then after about 100 yards you'll come to a fork..."

19

HISTORIC DEAL

Is that clear enough for everyone?

What exactly is 'Regulatory Alignment'?

THE Eye's helpful cut-out-and-keep guide for when you find yourself on the Irish Border (whether it be hard, soft or non-existent). 'Regulatory Alignment' is a common term:

Fudgetory Fudge	Mishy Mashification
Flimmity Flam	Blankety Blankment
Woollyish Wool	Flannely McFlannelface
Non-Specificatory Ambiguity	Spongebobificacious Squarepants

Er... Will this do? *(No – can you make it vaguer? Ed.)*

THOSE INSTITUTES IN FULL

Legatum Institute Sinister right-wing think tank dedicated to foreign affairs and exiting the EU – has links to Boris Johnson and Michael Gove

Legover Institute Not very sinister right-wing think tank dedicated to affairs with anyone available and exiting the bedroom before the husband gets home – has links to Boris Johnson, but you can't prove it

Lego Institute Sinister Danish think tank dedicated to building large pirate ships out of plastic bricks on Christmas morning – has links to itself, obviously, or you could not make anything

Legume Institute Sinister right-wing think tank dedicated to horticultural affairs and the removal of Brussels from public life – has links to top vegetables in Tory party

Legolas Institute Sinister Elvish think tank dedicated to Elvish affairs and effecting a hard exit from the Fellowship of the Ring – has links to Bilboris Baggins and the creepy Govelem *(That's enough institutes. Ed)*

"Stop talking it down – it's the wheel of the people"

K.J.Lamb

"Question everything, lad."

"Look- just fucking do it - OK?"

"Why?"

An Apology from the Daily Telegraph
Mrs Theresa May

WHEN we recently carried the headline on our front page "Blundering May Plunges Brexit into Shambolic Chaos" we may have given the impression that we in some way thought that the Prime Minister's conduct in the Brexit negotiations had not inspired in us total confidence that she knew what she was doing.

We now realise that, in light of the miraculous agreement that she reached with Mr Juncker at 4.30 in the morning, there was never a jot or tittle of truth in the above, and further, we now accept that Mrs May is a superb negotiator who knows exactly what she is doing, and that she has pulled off a diplomatic triumph of the highest order, by buying a little more time before having to get down to discussing all the really serious issues which next year threaten to plunge Britain's attempt to leave the EU into shambolic chaos.

Until that time, we are happy to offer Mrs May our profoundly insincere apologies, and to hail her as the greatest statesperson the world has ever known since Talleyrand, Metternich and Sir John Major KG, the hero of Maastricht.

Apology for the above apology

WHEN we hailed Mrs May as the greatest statesperson the world has ever known since Talleyrand, Metternich and Sir John Major KG, we may have somehow given the impression that she was a leader in full control of her party, who was in no circumstances about to lose the crucial vote about Brexit in the House of Commons.

We now realise that, in the light of her humiliating defeat by a treacherous coalition of Tory rebels and opportunistic Labour MPs, Mrs May is in fact a badly damaged Prime Minister, a dangerously weakened leader and little more than a dead woman walking.

Apology for the above apology for the apology above that

WHEN we cruelly described the Prime Minister as "a dead woman walking", we may have inadvertently led readers to believe that we considered her in no position to unite her party and lead her country out of Europe and into the sunlit uplands of a new and prosperous dawn for Britain, free from the shackles of a corrupt and decaying Euro-tyranny.

We now realise, in the light of nothing much happening and her having survived the weekend, despite a few attacks from Boris, Gove and the weasely Chancellor Hammond, that in fact Mrs May is exactly the leader we need to steady the ship... safe pair of shoes... strong and stable... greatest statesperson the world has ever known since Tallyho, Metternichtimothy and the hero of Maystrict, Sir John Mayjor NGG *(can I stop apologising and go on my Christmas holiday now? Ed.)*

Nursery Times

.... Friday, Once-upon-a-time ....

SOCIAL MEDIA THREATENS NURSERYLAND CHILDREN

by Our Online Correspondent **Tweetie Pie**

PARENTS were up in arms this week as Facestorybook launched their new platform aimed at children from 6-11 and adults from 18-94 pretending to be children from 6-11.

Said one concerned mother, "I sent Jack and Jill up the hill to fetch a pail of water, but Jack was so busy staring at his smart phone that he fell down and broke his crown, as well as the screen on his mobile. And Jill's no better – she came on Tumblr after."

Meanwhile, single parent Ms Horner said, "My boy Jack spends all day sitting in the corner Instagramming his Christmas Pie, and then adding 'thumbs down' emojis every time he pulls out a plum."

The concern is that children are spending so much time online nowadays that they are not enjoying healthy traditional Nurseryland pursuits like climbing beanstalks, stealing pigs and running away, and being eaten by witches.

"Children are simply growing up too fast now," said one father, a Mr Porgy. "My son Georgie was caught live-streaming the girls and making them cry.

"It's not his fault, it's the fault of the technological wizards behind the software, in particular that reclusive figure Mark Zuckerstiltskin – the evil genius behind Facestorybook – who is more interested in spinning gold than in the welfare of little babies!"

"Mum, Dad... I think I'm addicted to social media"

Does John Humphrys Really Work?

by **Walter Diviner**

Debate is raging over whether John Humphrys has any effect or whether he is just a superstitious relic from a bygone age.

When asked to confirm whether they were still actually using the ancient "Humphrys Method" on Radio 4 (which consists of shouting at people and interrupting them and going off on curious tangents), the BBC confirmed that Humphrys was one of a "broad range" of methods used, but that it was "by no means the only solution" to telling listeners what was going on.

Representatives from the British Society of Water Dowsers, Diviners and Equinoxal Witches announced that they, personally, felt that Humphrys was really useful, and that "even if you don't have proof that it's a good

thing, there's clearly something going on there, probably".

Scientists were keen to point out that multiple trials have found no evidence whatsoever that Humphrys has any positive effect on the listeners' mood in the morning, and that the substantial cost of Humphrys (estimated at £600,000 a year) means that other methods cannot be tried.

One said, "It's frankly completely backwards for a civilised nation still to be using this sort of thing. There must be a better way."

A Taxi Driver writes

EVERY week a well-known cab driver is invited to comment on an issue of topical importance. This week **John Worboys**, Prisoner Number F7832478.

Blimey! What's the world coming to, guv? They only

went and let me out on parole! And after only nine years? What a bloody disgrace! Here I am, back out on the streets, ready to start all over again! It's a joke, isn't it? Apparently, I've got religion. Pull the other one. No, they should string me up. It's the only language I understand. Fancy some champagne, darling? I've just been let out of prison and I'm celebrating! Talk about winning the lottery... *(That's not enough. Ed.)*

FROM THE ARCHIVES

THE DAILY NEWS
— 1948 —

NHS IN CRISIS

Health Service won't last winter, say doctors

Underfunding critical

Hospitals unable to cope

Australia win Ashes 4-0

VIRGIN TRAINS APOLOGISES FOR SEXIST LANGUAGE TO CUSTOMER

Nobody could possibly respect women more than I do

DIARY

MEGHAN MARKLE

Harry's family have all been so welcoming, reaching out to make me feel a very, very, special part of their family.

Three days ago, I met his Aunty Anne, and she was so intimate and cosy, full of real human warmth and understanding.

"Welcome aboard," she said, before turning around to greet one of her mother's corgis.

Two brief words.

But a whole world of compassion.

Harry's uncle Andrew is a beautiful person, too. He looked at me with those lovely wide eyes of his. I could tell he wanted to see the whole me, the real me, the me stripped of all the layers. And then he reached out and made a connection. The human touch is so important.

Then he used one of those lovely old English expressions I'd never heard before. "You're a bit of all right," he said. Harry later told me it signified a deep and enduring appreciation of who I am and where I come from.

And Harry's beloved gramps Pip is so sweet and natural and awesome: overflowing with the wisdom of years. I thought he seemed so old he must even, like, remember The Beatles. Had he ever met them? The way he told it, they were like fresh rain sent by the heavens to nurture our planet. "An absolute shower," he told me. Poetry flows through those elderly veins.

We exchanged wisdom. I said that sending love and good vibes and positivity into our universe is, for me, the only thing in this life that truly matters. He told me that, for him, it was vital to have a good, strong handshake, to speak up, and to look the other person fairly and squarely in the eye.

He seemed so vulnerable, almost – how shall I put this? – like a little kid who's lost his way. I so wanted to bring him out of his shell, to put him at his ease.

"All that matters is that you be YOU!" I said. "That's the greatest contribution to humanity that any of us can ever make. Follow this rule, and your footstep on this, our planet, will be profound. After all, it's the only one we have."

He went silent. I knew he was lost in thought, imbibing the truth in my words.

"Shall we go through?" he said. Just four short words. But so deeply profound.

I can't believe how authentic The Queen is. No wonder her family nickname is "Her Majesty"! Well-deserved? You bet!

Whatever she does, wherever she goes, she's just so refreshingly AUTHENTIC. There's no other word for it. Like the great Meryl Streep, who she's clearly learnt so much from, she invests profound time and energy into being authentic. And that's something I respect.

Another literally amazing thing about The Queen (my grandmom-in-law-to be!!) is that, even at her venerable age, she's always so willing to LEARN.

Only last week, she was telling me about her "Christmas message", where the networks offer her ten minutes prime-time to talk freely about the things that are troubling her.

I thought, maybe she's, well, not envious exactly, because believe me, she's not that kind of person, but, like, maybe she's thinking it would be nicer in some ways to have the 44 minutes a week we get to have on Suits, and I wanted to be totally positive, so I was saying, like "CONGRATULATIONS! I mean, ten minutes is literally AMAZING! You should be so PROUD of that! I mean, there's so much you can DO in ten minutes! It's a great platform!"

We made such a connection. Like me, she's really proud of who she is and where she comes from. And – also like me! – she's passionate about broadcasting, and yearns to focus her energies on just getting better and better. And that's so inspiring.

"I so want you to tell me all about your Christmas show!" I said to her. She told me she just looks to the camera and keeps talking!

"Wow! That's great!" I said. And she looked so happy.

Encouragement means so much to us. I think it was Mahatma Gandhi who said, "Don't be the reason someone feels insecure. Be the reason someone feels seen, heard, and supported by the whole universe." And that's always been my watchword.

But I also knew that, as I say, Elizabeth loves to learn. So I touched her gently on her beautiful old wrist and I said, "You know what? You've developed such a totally AMAZING show. And there was me thinking SUITS was long-running! So who am I to offer advice!!!?!!!"

At that point she gave me a lovely, soft, gentle, almost beseeching look. It seemed to shout, "Hey there! All tips welcome, Meghan! Together, let's turn this show around!"

So I told her that maybe it could be even more amazing if she didn't just launch straight into her monologue, great though it is, like maybe she should make it a teensy bit more inclusive and introduce the show by stretching out her arms and welcoming viewers "to our beautiful home here in London, England".

You know what? She looked so hungry to learn. As an actress, I've made a lifelong study of my fellow human beings. I've developed a – I don't know – call it a "sixth sense". I don't know how, but I instantly identified that "tell me more!" look in her eyes.

As told to
CRAIG BROWN

THOROUGHLY MODERN ME

(surely 'Meghan'? Ed)

INDIA TRIGHT

WHO IS SHE?

She is strong, opinionated and full of aplomb. Yes, she's me. *(Surely "Meghan" again? Ed.)* You can imagine what it meant for Meghan when she first saw the photo-byline of a mixed-race, divorced, independent career woman who has made it to the very top of the page – me.

When she looks at me, Meghan sees a fully adult, articulate, charming, brown person and not some inbred aristo or hulking great Sloane filling up the pages of the Sunday Times.

No, I represent the future and Meghan must have been delighted to find that just by filling up the pages of a national newspaper, I have made a huge difference to *(We get the idea. Ed)*

The Christine Keeler I Knew
by A.Chair

Well, it was obviously a bit embarrassing, as we were both naked, but I remember she was very nice and put me at my ease. When she sat on me she joked that I had better legs than her! And everyone laughed. I think she made sure I was alright when we finished, which was very nice of her.

It was a fun thing to do, but obviously it put an end to any dreams I had for a serious career. I had hoped that the fame would catapult me into the West End and I would get sat on by a Jimmy Porter or perhaps even, one day, a Hamlet (in a Trevor Nunn modernist interpretation you understand!) but alas, I was forever known as "the Chair that Naked Bird sat on".

I did a few Carry Ons (Barbara Windsor stood on me so Sid James could look up her skirt) and Frank Spencer fell off me in an episode of 'Some Mothers Do 'Ave Em', but I'm afraid the only things I was offered were 'Furniture Nasties' and the odd DFS advert, but I'm happy to have had my moment in the *(cont. p94)*

ENGLAND FACE TOUGHEST TEST YET
by Our Test Match Special Team
Aggers, Staggers and **Chunders**

WITH two tests down, the England team arrives in Perth confronted with the biggest challenge in Ashes history.

Can they stay sober long enough to take to the field? The omens don't look good, with Perth bars open and ready to serve a variety of alcoholic beverages long into the night.

Can Root and his men buckle down, concentrate and avoid getting into fights with Australians or with each other?

They know it's a big ask and they will have to answer some searching questions if they are to make it through the Perth test at the Wacca. Questions such as: "What are you having?", "Would you like another?", "Haven't you had enough?", "Did you spill my pint?", "Do you want to come outside?" and "When's the next plane home?".

Said former England top drinker, Phil Glass *(surely "Tufnell"? Ed)*, "It's all about bottle. The lads have got to dig deep and be careful with their shot selection – whisky, vodka and flaming Drambuie are too risky at this stage of the series.

"If they can make it through the first session at Dingo's Booze Shack (9pm-5am), they're in with a chance of turning up to the ground and getting thoroughly beaten."

Ben Drunkett is 23.

I want the businesses to live on after I die... so I'm selling them to someone else

---

POETRY CORNER

In Memoriam Christine Keeler, 1942-2017

So. Farewell
Then Christine Keeler,
You were most
Famous for going to
Bed with War Minister
John Profumo and
Bringing down the
Government of
Harold Macmillan.

This launched the
Swinging Sixties when
Everyone was allowed
To go to bed with
Everyone else,
Except you
And Mr Profumo,
Obviously.

       E.J. Thribb (17½)

THEATRE NEWS

Hamiltons

IT'S the show we've all been waiting for. People are paying up to 20p to see the top musical that took Broadway (Hammersmith) by storm: 'Hamiltons'.

The story takes place in that epic period of political upheaval which saw the creation of a new government, and follows Neil Hamilton's meteoric political career from disgraced Tory MP, all the way to the giddy heights of leader of the Welsh branch of UKIP.

Always by his side or behind him in the panto horse is the woman he loves, Christine. The music in Hamiltons is a mixture of true blues, flip flop and House (of Commons).

Hit numbers include: *Put it on the Ritz, Knees Up Mother Brown Envelope, Goodness Gracious Great Balls of Fayed*, and many others.

TV HIGHLIGHTS

The Crown

(Netflix Episode 94)

It is 1957 and the rocky marriage of the Queen and the Duke of Edinburgh continues, as Prince Philip admits to an affair with Christine Keeler while on an official visit to Berlin to meet his relatives Prince Adolph of Hitlerberg and Princess Eva von Braunshirt.

The young queen is devastated by Philip's betrayal and takes it out on the prime minister, Sir Anthony Armstrong Eden, rudely demanding that he shave off his moustache before marrying her sister, Princess Margaret Thatcher.

Meanwhile, the young Prince Charles has been sent to the brutal Scottish public school, Gordonbrown, where the sadistic headmaster, Mr McHimmler, an old German friend of Prince Philip, insists that he runs a steeplechase up Ben Fogle in midwinter wearing nothing but a sporran.

Traumatised, Charles complains to his icy mother who immediately tells his strict father who then asks the headmaster to beat Charles to death with a claymore.

Meanwhile, the Suez crisis reaches a highpoint as Lord Mountbatten's torrid affair with President Nasser is hushed up by the new government of Harold McWilson... *(to be continued)*.

EYE RATING: First-rate performances by the Queen as Clare Foy and Dr Who as Prince Philip, aided by painstaking research by writer Peter Moreplease, make this the must-watch TV of the week.

Sylvanian Family

Trans Sylvanian Family

Your New Caring, Sharing Feminist
Daily Mail
COMMENT

BBC sexism 'slammed'

THERE is rightfully a sense of disbelief following the shock resignation of the BBC's China editor Carrie Gracie over the BBC's "secret and illegal pay culture", in which women earn significantly less than their male counterparts.

How could the BBC treat one of its finest journalists in such a disgraceful sexist way? A journalist so committed to her work that she lives 5,000 miles away from her two teenage children, two children cared for back in London by her ex-husband, a Chinese rock drummer called Jin who speaks no English?

How dare the BBC treat this absent mother in a flagrantly sexist manner, a woman who has surrendered her precious babies into the care of a man barely able to communicate with them?

A woman putting her career ahead of her most basic desires to nurture and care for her children should not expect to be treated in this sexist manner, and we at the *Daily Mail* are standing shoulder to shoulder with this evil, callous, careerist, man-hating, trouser-suit-wearing bitch queen with her impassioned plea that speaks of fairness, justice and how terrible the BBC is and how it should be shut down to allow rivals like the Mail Online to take over the entire *(cont. p94)*

"Here's some of my salary... go buy yourself something nice"

Monday January 8th

INNER WORKINGS REVEALED

THE Chinese people were today afforded a rare glimpse inside the secretive inner workings of the labyrinthine-like BBC senior management, after the purging of the China editor Carrie Gracie.

"BBC management retains the same top down hierarchical structure which has served it well for many decades, with senior managers maintaining strict centralised control through a culture of fear and reprisals within individual departments," said one fascinated Chinese Communist party official.

"This works to stifle dissent. As lowly reporters know, if you try to break ranks and speak out about your salary, you will find yourself exiled and presenting News24 at 3am or worse 'Farming Today'.

"Sexism is rife within this rigid corporation structure, with women earning far less and the most senior positions all being filled by men in suits who look identical."

GLENDA SLAGG
She's Fleet Street's Fire and Fury!!??!!

■ HENRY BOLTON!!??!! What a sleazy love-rat!!?!! He's Ukip's new leader, or should I say Leaver (Geddit!!?), who's dumped his foreign missus in order to Ukip(!!) with a younger model half his age!!?!?!! Who does he think he is – Nigel Farage???!?!! And Horny Henry only got the job 'cos he was meant to be a safe pair of hands!?! Safe pair of wandering hands more like!!??! They should send you back home, Mr Bonking Bolton, except poor old Tatiana Smurova-Bolton has probably changed the locks?!!!?! Geddit!!?!!

■ HATS and trousers off to Ukip's latest love machine!?!! Henry Bolton I'm talking about, Mister!!!??! OK, so he's done the dirty on three wives already – one Danish fancy and two Russian dolls – but at least he's now shacked up with a British blonde!!?! And she's got the same views on immigration as he has!!?! No wonder Ukip's Mr Big Boy found the twenty-year-old topless totty so attractive!!?! It's clearly a meeting of minds!!? Good luck to Jo Marney, or should I say ex-Mrs Bolton Number Four??!! Geddit??!!

■ SEEN McMAFIA??!!! Apparently the Russians are taking over everything!!? Especially the telly, the newspapers and even Auntie Glenda's column?!! Z-Z-Z-Z-Z-Z-Z-Z-Z-Z-ski!?!?

■ WATCH all the sisters at the Golden Globes??!! #MeMeMeMe MeMeMe(Too). Just sayin'!!!?!

■ *HERE THEY ARE – Glenda's All-Female Big Brothers?!?!*
● **Joe Root!?!!** OK, he's not female but nor is everyone on Big Brother!??!! Poor old Joe is feeling sick to his boots!!? Not as sick as we are, watching his shambles of a team flopping to cr-Ashes defeat!!?? (Geddit??!!)
● **Mason Crane!?!** OK, he's not female either but he's the new English leg spin bowler!??!! He's certainly bowled this maiden over and I'm spinning with (*This is terrible. Ed.*)
● **Steve Smith!?!** OK, so the Australian captain is still not a woman but at least he's on top Down Under!??!! And that's the way Auntie Glenda likes it!!! (*This is worse than watching the All-Female Big Brother. You're fired and I'm furious. Ed.*)

Byeee!!

THOSE KEY MOMENTS WHERE ENGLAND LOST THE ASHES

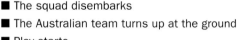

■ Their plane lands in Australia
■ The squad disembarks
■ The Australian team turns up at the ground
■ Play starts
■ Er…
■ That's it.

Who do you think should be the next girlfriend of the Ukip leader?
You choose who should occupy the nation's number one hottie-seat!

Katie Hopkins

Kellyanne Conway

Cruella de Vil

Toby Young

Grace Mugabe

Eva Braun

Jo Marney again

WHITE HOUSE BOOK FURY

Trump tells lawyers to close stable doors and sue horse

DONALD Trump has announced his determination to sue the horse who has written an extraordinary book alleging chaos in the White House.

In a late-night phone rant to his chief of staff, Trump ordered the National Guard be deployed to "close the stable doors, right now, seriously, I mean this minute, I don't want them open a second longer, we are getting on top of this situation", while disregarding the fact that the horse has been running around doing interview shows on morning television and flogging his book.

A spokesman for the White House announced that, "In order not to give this horse any more publicity, President Trump is today launching an enormous campaign via his Twitter feed saying 'Do Not Listen To The Horse, The Horse Is Fake, Everyone Pay No Further Attention To The Horse', accompanied by a picture of the horse and a link to the book's page on Amazon."

Said the President, "The book stops here!" Like many of his announcements, this turned out not to be true.

Revealed: Genius method used by inspired, prize-winning journalist Michael Wolff to gain unparalleled access to the White House

● Sit in the White House
● Ask President if you can write a no-holds-barred book about him full of juicy details
● President will not listen to you and will say "sure, whatever"
● Write book.

The Eye's Controversial New Columnist

This week I am very angry about the salacious book *The Fury and the Baby* that's been written about me. This has made me so angry! And what has made me even angrier is my thumbs haven't developed enough to allow me to tweet angrily about it. There are many shock allegations in this book, notably the fact that I watch CBeebies all day, I go to bed around four o'clock in the afternoon, I throw my toys all over the floor, I eat Nutella and mashed banana before falling asleep, and I refuse to read anything longer than a *Spot the Dog* book. All these allegations are true, granted, but what I resent is the insinuation that all these habits make me somehow unsuitable to be the world's leading baby! This aspect of "fake news" is very disturbing, and as soon as my mother finishes reading this disgraceful book to me, I will comb the few strands of hair over my naked scalp and make a furious statement via my Fisher-Price microphone, if I'm able to stay awake long enough to (cont. p94)

Please can we come in?

Why I was wrong to ever doubt Jeremy Corbyn, despite him not winning the general election and messing it up for another five years

 by Our Political Correspondents
Owen Goal and Zoe Willthisdo

A lot of people have said that perhaps it was wrong of me to suggest, in recent articles on him which are annoyingly still available on Google, that Jeremy Corbyn was a "waste of space, a hopeless, useless void completely divorced from political reality who should be chopped immediately if we ever want the party to win an actual majority at an actual election."

I would just like to further explain what I meant by that statement, which is that – of course – I think Jeremy is the best leader Labour have ever had, even though he didn't technically "win" last year's election. Here's why:

● He's swept to victory in two out of three of the elections he has fought (OK, two were party leadership and the one he didn't win was the general election, but still)

● He has record levels of popularity among people who care about internal Labour party politics, which is an enormous and growing number of people, possibly outnumbering even the electorate

● He will still be younger than 75 by the time of the next election, which is years younger than Churchill was when he became PM for the second time. And what did Churchill ever achieve before 1951?

In short, I would like to publicly admit that, even though I have always loved Big Brother Jeremy, my means of expressing this love has been imperfect.

Furthermore, there has been lots of talk of me being a "Blairite scumbag", whereas in fact I have written below a list of people who are actual Blairites and whom we should persecute instead of me. They are: 1) Tony Blair, 2) Alastair Campbell, 3) Tony Blair again, the Blairite scumbag, 4) (*That's enough scumbags. Ed.*)

LOOKS LIKE TOM & DICK WILL BE THERE AS WELL AS HARRY

PUBLIC INVITED TO ROYAL WEDDING

ROBERT THOMPSON

Trump declares Moscow capital of United States

by Our Foreign Affairs Staff
Jerry Salem and **Tel Aviv**

THE President of the United States has yet again confounded the international community by making a controversial presidential proclamation by tweet.

In the early hours of yesterday morning, while making his way back from the toilet, Donald Trump told his 44 million followers, "This makes sense. From now on, Moscow is the Capital of the United States. Everyone knows it is. Quit pretending! #Realnews."

The relocation of America's capital city from Washington to Moscow is a huge undertaking which has widespread ramifications throughout the world.

Not everyone was pleased, and the United Nations said that it could destabilise the world as we know it. The UN prefers a two-state solution with the US and Russia as two separate countries rather than as one big melting pot of two conflicting ideologies.

But Trump supporters were quick to back the president's inflammatory gesture, saying, "Just look online, everyone's in favour of it, including Putinbot742 who has retweeted 'Make Moscow Great Again' three billion times."

HOW IT WILL LOOK: THE RED HOUSE

Jerusalem 'is capital of England' claim

by Our Romantic Poetry Staff
Wanda Cloud and **Dafydd Dyll**

THE late William Blake has stepped into the controversial row over the question of Jerusalem being the capital of the state of Israel. "Everyone knows that Jerusalem was builded here, in England's green and pleasant land."

Mr Blake continued to explain his theory which involved Glastonbury, Joseph of Aramathea and the planting of a thorn bush, saying, "Mine is the correct version. We all know that Jerusalem is situated right smack off the A532, just before the Sword-in-Hand services at Junction 6, amongst the dark satanic mills.

"Trump's behaviour defines him as a ranting madman, who has clearly fallen for an old myth. You might almost," he quipped, "call it fayke news."

Mr Blake is of course most famous for his poem, "And did those tweets in ancient time".

Film highlights

Coming soon:
Job the builder

It's Job's biggest job yet, as he gets the contract to build the new American Embassy in the middle of Jerusalem. Laugh along with Job as Bully the Bulldozer takes time off from destroying the homes of Palestinians and building settlements to clear the way for Job's challenging new project.

It's going to require all of Job's patience, as well as a hard hat at all times, not to mention full body armour, especially during tea breaks.

There'll be lots of Job's other friends there – including Benjamin the tank, Benjamin the other tank, and Benjamin the other three hundred tanks, personnel carriers and numerous other military vehicles. What a busy day it will be for Amy the Ambulance.

Sing along with Job's theme tune: "Can they bomb it? Yes – they probably can."

PRESIDENTIAL TERMS – A BRIEF HISTORY

Shithole

Shithead

Just to be clear, I never liked Woody Allen

By Ann Actor, Ann Otheractor, and Ann Y-onewhoknowswhatsgoodforthem

A lot of people have been suggesting that I in some way approve of Woody Allen, or even that I've worked with him in the past.

This regrettable allegation has been aired because I happened to appear in minor starring roles in three of his films within five years. It may also have been because of comments I may (or may not) have made in interviews after some of our previous collaborations, including: "He's just the finest director working today, a Bergman of the human psyche" or "I wept with respect when I saw his inspired editing of the tasteful shots of my cleavage" or "Woody's new film, *Older Professor Beds 25-Year-Old Student*, is this year's *Citizen Kane* and deserves every single Oscar available".

I now realise, on the strength of allegations of child abuse which have been around for many years but have recently resurfaced with added cultural cachet, that Woody Allen is the devil himself *(cont. p94)*

(cont. p94)

"Go away, I'm not who you think I am"

Letters to the Editor

Not Our Finest Hour

SIR – As lifelong admirers of the late Sir Winston Churchill, undoubtedly the greatest British prime minister of this or any other age, my wife and I recently drove into Market Barkworth to attend a cinematic performance of the new film "Darkest Hour".

Imagine our horror on discovering that this supposed account of the momentous events of 1940, which Lady Letitia and I remember as if it was yesterday, was nothing but a complete travesty of the historical facts.

Not five minutes into the film, we were shown footage of what purported to be a typical London street of the time, in which one could clearly see, driving along in the background, a 1953 Ford Consul.

In another scene, barely an hour later, we were further subjected to a scene in which a Wren is seen typing in the Cabinet War Room when a Rear-Admiral passes her desk on his way to see Mr Churchill (as he then was).

The Wren fails to jump to her feet to salute her senior officer, which at the time would have been a disciplinary offence, possibly leading to a court martial.

So much for the claim by the makers of this ridiculous farrago of blatant factual errors that they had employed a team of military experts to ensure that every historical detail was correct.

At least the film was redeemed by the one inspiring scene where Churchill is shown as having doubts as to whether Britain should continue to fight the Nazis or sue for peace.

Wanting to know which course the British people would wish him to take, Churchill enters the carriage of an underground train where he seeks the views of a typical cross-section of ordinary 1940 Britons. They include a chimney sweep called "Bert", a children's nanny who gives her name

as "Miss Poppins", a cloth-capped dustman, Mr Doolittle, and his charming daughter, Eliza, who works as a flower girl, and then, to complete the picture of how our country looked in those days, several representatives of Britain's then worldwide empire, including a turbanned Sikh, a stern-looking Imam and a West Indian expert on British and Roman history, all of whom are shown conducting an animated discussion with on Britain's military options with gallant members of London's wartime LGBTQ community.

Quite rightly, they all end up shouting "Go for it, Winnie, kick that Hitler in the goolies, the nation is right behind you".

As they all produce Union Jacks from their pockets to sing a rousing chorus of "Rule Britannia", the Prime Minister bursts into tears and then strides off to the House of Commons to deliver the speech which undoubtedly won the war.

Sir Herbert Gussett
Dunsurrenderin,
St Andalone, Dorset

How Hitler would put it today

"We must liberate the British from the fascist, racist Churchill!"

IRAN CRISIS – NOW MODERATE ROUHANI STEPS IN

by Our Middle East Staff **Terry Rahn**

AS Iran continues to be riven by nationwide protests, with tens of thousands of demonstrators taking to the streets in cities across the land, the country's moderate, liberal, reformist President, Hassan Rouhani, last night intervened to restore calm to the increasingly turbulent public mood.

In a conciliatory television address, Mr Rouhani assured the Iranian people that they had every right to protest and make their views known.

"Iran," he insisted, "is proud of being a democratic republic, and it is very important for people to be able to offer constructive criticism of the government, which can help to improve the efficient running of the nation.

"However," he went on, as he was joined by a number of armed members of the much-respected Islamic Revolutionary Community Police, "there can be no justification for criticising the Islamic religion.

"Those who have been protesting that there is too much unemployment in Iran, or that nobody's pensions have been paid, are clearly offering a direct and unforgiveable insult to the Prophet Mohammed, and this criminal behaviour is wholly unacceptable in a civilised modern theocracy like the Islamic Republic of Iran."

As the great reformer's voice rose in a menacing crescendo, he further emphasised that those protestors who complain that they are starving to death while their government spends billions on propping up the Assad regime in Syria are "committing blasphemy and sacrilege of a type which is only punishable by a wholesale programme of mass executions".

At this point, the champion of a liberal way forward for Iran explained that those who argued that not everyone who disagreed with the Ayatollah Khamenei should be killed are failing to realise that Iran's much-respected prisons are already at bursting point, with so many ordinary citizens doing all they can to get into them.

"There is simply no more room," he added, "for any more of these blaspheming demonstrators to be housed a the state's expense.

"The only humane solution to this problem," a sombre President Rouhani concluded, "is for all these infidel puppets of the Great Satan Trump to be hanged from cranes outside every mosque in Iran."

Daily Mail, Friday, January 26, 2018

Sarah Vain

How I lost 94 stone without even trying because I'm so great

BEFORE

AFTER

IT'S incredible – I didn't go on a mad diet, do punishing exercise or have invasive surgery. All I did was simply have a haircut, put on some different clothes and persuade the *Daily Mail* to give me an entire page to go on about myself. Amazing! And that's just me *(cont. p94, 95, 96)*

GOVERNMENT DEFENDS CARILLION COLLAPSE

> Outsourcing works extremely well

WERE THE CRACKS ALWAYS VISIBLE?

HS2 PROJECT 'NOT UNDER THREAT'

by Our Infrastructure Staff **U Plonker**

DOWNING Street says it has moved quickly in the wake of the Carillion collapse to ensure there is no delay to HS2 by retendering the two HS2 deals, with the contract going to the well-respected construction firm, "Trotters Independent Traders".

"The taxpayer can be assured that the retendering process was conducted with all the same rigour and due diligence as the original awarding of the contract to Carillion," said a Downing Street spokesman.

"We see Trotters Independent Traders as the right company to

deliver this complex project on time and under budget."

A spokesman for Trotters Independent Traders described winning the HS2 contract as "lovely jubbly", adding, "This time next year, Rodders, we'll be billionaires."

MGBLGBTQ

EveningStandard
Friday 26 January 2018

WHO'S TO BLAME FOR CARILLION DISASTER?

by Our Entire Staff

NOW, as the dust settles after the dreadful collapse of construction giant Carillion, we must start the search to discover who exactly is responsible for the terrible mess, thanks to the government outsourcing everything to dodgy firms who claimed they could do everything far more cheaply than was possible.

The Evening Standard's editorial team have analysed the whole story closely and, based on up to 20 seconds of intensive study, we can reveal that the blame lies entirely with the Prime Minister.

Mrs May was quite clearly the only one saying we should work with Carillion and and it was she who came up with the whole stupid idea in the first place.

Where the blame clearly does **not** lie is with anyone who preceded her in Number 10 or Number 11 Downing Street – if anyone can remember who those people even were – because it doesn't matter, as it's definitely Theresa's fault and she should never have sacked me and that should be an end to the matter, all right?

Notes&queries

What is Carillion?

● A "carillion" is, as every medieval scholar knows, a collection of bells hung in a cathedral tower to be rung at special events, including Saints days, outbreaks of plague and foreign invasions. Derived from the old French word "quadrillon" (literally, "a clanger"), this four-bell assemblage was a distinct feature of provincial towns in the Jean-Lainguedoc until unwise expansion led to carillions being loaded with more and more bells until the tower at St-Uppidie-Este, with its one and a half billion bells, collapsed, destroying the entire village and most of the surrounding countryside.
Rev. J. McAlpine.

● Oh dear, oh dear. The good Reverend has made a bit of a "clanger" himself here. Carillion is, of course, a famous 1980s prog rock band whose name derived from the fantasy novels of J.R.R. Toksvig, particularly the late work "The Carillion". Popular in Japan, the band, led by lead singer "Fishy", reached number 94 in the international LP charts in 1987 with their concept album "The Outsource Kingdom", including the single "Making tomorrow a better place"). This, sadly, was followed by the break-up of the band, which left the members in extended litigation over their £1.5bn debts. "Fishy" (real name Jim Tarmac) now works in the track maintenance department of HS2.
Major General Sir John Laing.

● One hopes that the Major General knows more about warfare than he does about etymology. Carillion, for heaven's sake, is a colour. You'll find it on the pantone chart (no. 1.5 billion) and it is a shade of very deep red, which the novelist Charles Dickens frequently used viz "The faces of the assembled drinkers that night in the Builders Arms public house were as carillion in hue as a baboon's bottom on the Barbary Coast" *(The Pickwick Paupers).*
Mrs Mo Mowlam.

● Please, please, no more, Mo! Has no one read "Captain Carillion's Mandolin", the story of a man whose badly constructed musical instrument falls apart, as *(That's enough. Ed.)*

DIARY

MARY BERRY'S HOUSEHOLD TIPS

If you tend to feel the cold, why not invest in an extra blanket?

When the time comes for choosing a new sofa, remember that a very large sofa may not fit into a very small room. On the other hand, a very small sofa will almost certainly fit into a very large room, but it's all a matter of personal taste.

Keys. Hang your front door keys inside the door, not outside, or burglars may use them to gain entry.

Personally, I always prefer a nice soft sofa to a rock-hard one, but that's just a matter of taste. Sofas stuffed with feathers tend to be softer than those stuffed with something harder, such as iron, rocks, or household implements.

Cupboards are ideal for putting things in. They generally come with a door, or even two doors, so they can be shut when not "in use". For instructions on how to shut your own particular cupboard, refer to the manufacturer's guidelines.

The marvellous thing about a mirror is that it enables you to see your own face in it, looking back at you. And the same thing applies to other people too, of course!

Adding mushrooms to stock gives it a lovely mushroomy flavour.

A garlic press is excellent if you want to press garlic, but I find it not quite so good for wiping sticky surfaces.

The best way to follow a recipe is from start to finish. If you start at the end, you may find yourself taking all your ingredients out of the oven before you have mixed them together or cooked them.

Flowers always brighten a room. Try placing them on a table rather than on the floor, where they might be knocked over. I always think they look at their best with their polythene wrapping removed, though this is a matter of personal taste.

Before giving a dinner party, consider how many people you want to invite. Too few can be not quite enough, and too many can be rather too many. Sitting twenty or more guests around a table designed for four may prove a bit of a squeeze.

Shopping is quite an art in itself! Butchers are wonderful places for finding meat, whilst vegetables are readily available at most greengrocers.

Caring for shoes. If it's raining and muddy, then it's best to wear something waterproof, such as wellingtons. Wellington boots are generally considered unsuitable for smart dinner parties or society balls, but, if you must wear them on these occasions, do give them a good wipe first.

When eating a boiled egg, be careful to remove the shell first, or it can be too crunchy.

Things that shouldn't go in the dishwasher: cutlery with bone handles, china with gold or silver detailing, velvet cushions, fresh flowers, household pets, large items of furniture.

Leftover gravy can be very useful for getting rid of red wine stains. Just spread two or three gallons of leftover gravy evenly across your carpet, and the wine stain will disappear beneath

the rough brown hue. And the smell will get those tastebuds going!

Never take anything piping hot out of the oven with your bare hands, or you may suffer serious burns. I swear by "oven gloves", and like to place one over each hand. Placing both hands in the same glove can sometimes make things tricky to handle. So I place my left hand in the left glove and my right hand in the right glove, but it's very much a matter of personal taste!

Bookshelves are perfect for storing books. I place mine on the shelf with the spine facing outwards. This lets me see what the book is without having to pull it out.

Most books are numbered at the bottom of each page, so you can tell at a glance what page you are on. To keep the flow going, books are best read in the order of the numbers at the bottom of the page.

Fireplaces. Before making a fire in your living room, first make sure you have a fireplace. A roaring fire lit any-old-where in your living room can seriously damage your carpets and furniture.

The hallway is an excellent place for storing umbrellas. I always put my umbrellas "down" before storing them indoors, as it leaves more space. But this is very much a matter of taste.

Packing your suitcase. If you are going somewhere hot, it's unwise to pack too many woolly jumpers or anoraks. On the other hand, if you're going somewhere cold and wet, you don't want to be caught with only a t-shirt or skimpy top! I always look and see where I am going before setting off, and then pick my clothes accordingly.

As told to

CRAIG BROWN

School news

St Cakes

Hijab term (formerly Hilary Term) resumes today. There are 158 boys in the school and some girls sitting quietly in another building. The Headmistress, Ms Ima Moderate, has been replaced by Ms Sharia Law, who has the full confidence of the governors under their new chairman, Mr John Jihadi. The curriculum will now concentrate on the three Rs – Religion, Religion and Religion.

The Behead Boy is Al Kyder (Radicals) and the Coverthehead Girl is Donna Burker (White Widows). Fastings will be held on 14 March 1439AH. The school play, *Lady Windermere's Fanatic* by Oscar Wilde, will be performed in the new school mosque (formerly the IT Centre). The Tug of Holy War (formerly Sports Day) will take place on Martyrs' Day. *(That's enough. Ed.)*

Fine Dining

TORIES – THE FUTURE

We must throw off the shackles of the EU and trade freely again with Persia, Mesopotamia and Cathay

---

'Why Capita is totally different from Carillion' explains Capita boss

by Our Business Staff
P.F.I. Friday

THE Chief Executive of the beleaguered outsourcing giant, Capita, today hit back at the multi-billion-pound company's detractors by explaining why his business has nothing in common with the failed outsourcing giant, Carillion.

Said Mr Jonathan Suit, who has recently stepped up to replace Nick Suit, who took over from Andy Suit, "It is quite ridiculous to draw any comparisons whatsoever between Capita and Carillion, apart from the fact that they both begin with the same two letters. Otherwise there is no similarity at all between our own hugely successful business operation, which just happens to be going through a little bit of temporary turbulence, and the hopelessly incompetent and mismanaged disaster that was Carillion."

Mr Suit then listed all the ways in which the two firms were entirely dissimilar.

"First," he said, "Carillion had allowed its debts to run totally out of control, whereas ours are only very modest, which is why we are having a rights issue, asking for £700 million.

"Secondly, Carillion had completely failed to look after its pension fund, meaning that tens of thousands of its pensioners would be left high and dry, whereas our pension fund deficit is only a mere £380 million.

"Thirdly, Carillion had taken on an absurdly inflated and ridiculous array of government services, ranging from building HS2 and PFI-funded hospitals, to running public libraries.

"We at Capita, on the other hand, have a very logical portfolio of government services, ranging from running the London congestion charge, the jobseekers' allowance helpline and the collection of council business rates, to helping the BBC with answering complaints.

"Fourthly, Carillion was well aware that it was heading for one of the most humiliating bankruptcies in Britain's history, despite continuing to hand out millions of pounds in dividends to its shareholders, not to mention its vastly overpaid directors and senior staff.

"With shameless cynicism, it even issued a severe profits warning, in the full knowledge that it no longer had anything like enough money to honour all its commitments, which was enough to send its share price plummeting through the floor.

"None of this, of course," he went on, "bears any resemblance to the situation we are facing here at Capita where... let me just answer this phone, please... oh my God... surely not... is that really right?"

At this point, Mr Suit was unavailable for further comment.

A+E

"Been waiting long?"

BROOIG

MARVELLOUS MEGHAN IS ROYAL BREATH OF FRESH AIR! p1

PUSHY STARLET TURNS HALLOWED TRADITION ON ITS HEAD p2

MAGNIFICENT MARKLE TRANSFORMS ROYAL STYLE p3

WANNABE ACTRESS FLAUNTS RED CARPET FLESH p4

KATE LOOKS FORWARD TO WONDERFUL MAY WEDDING DAY p5

MANIPULATIVE MARKLE STEALS KATE'S THIRD-BABY THUNDER p6

CARING KATE LOSES A BROTHER-IN-LAW BUT GAINS A SISTER p7

MINXY MEG CRASHES ROYAL INNER CIRCLE – IN HER DREAMS!?! p8

MATURE MEGHAN TAMES WILD HARRY p9

ICE QUEEN KILLS HARRY'S FUN-ATICAL FREE SPIRIT p10

MEDIA-SAVVY MEG PREPARED FOR PRESS BLITZ p11

SELF-PUBLICISING HARPY STEALS ROYAL LIMELIGHT p12

MATERNAL MEG BRINGS WEALTH OF EXPERIENCE p13

DESPERATE DIVORCEE SNARES RICH SUCKER p14

MIXED-RACE MEGHAN IS NEW FACE OF ROYALTY p15

YES, SHE'S STRAIGHTENED HER HAIR AND HAD A NOSE JOB p16

JOYOUS WEDDING PREPARATIONS BEGIN p17

WE PREPARE TO DIG UP DIRT AND PUT THE BOOT IN p18

MATCHING COUPLE SHARE FAMILY HEARTBREAK p19

BOTH THEIR DADS ARE LOONIES – ESPECIALLY HERS! p20

MEGA MEGHAN CAN SAVE THE HOUSE OF WINDSOR p21

HOUSE PRICES TO COLLAPSE – STARTING WITH WINDSOR p22

Moron interviews Moron

Those killer questions posed in the historic Trump interview

1. Are you, as some people say, an idiot who is unfit for your job?

2. Are you a feminist or, in fact, a misogynist?

3. Why do you keep saying you are very popular in Britain when all the evidence suggests everyone hates you?

4. Will you apologise for those fake photos in the Daily Mirror? (*Is this right? Ed.*)

CAR MAKERS ADMIT THEY TESTED EFFECTS OF DIESEL EXHAUST ON SIMPLE PRIMATES

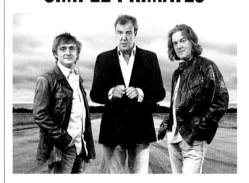

Hello, do you sell divers' watches?

No, I'm afraid we only sell the one type

Moose Allain

From The Message Boards

Members of the online community respond to the major issues of the day...

'Racist' pub probe

Guys, I see that an investigation is underway into an Essex pub which has a display of 15 golliwogs (some of which appear to be hanging from cords). The suggestion is that it's racist, but the landlord insists he welcomes customers of all races, and says the toys were gifts from customers. I must admit it's never occurred to me to offer a golly (or any other gift) to a pub landlord. Maybe that's why I always seem to get served last! – *Bogbrush*

I have offered golliwogs to no fewer than 27 landlords and landladies in the past week. All refused, using pusillanimous excuses such as, 'It's company policy to not accept gifts.' Some of these pubs, incidentally, had changed their traditional names (The Blackie Boy, The Blackamoor, etc). – *Relf was Right*

May I ask why you did this? – *Bogbrush*

As my name should tell you, I am a longstanding supporter of freedom. When shopping in branches of 'our' leading supermarket, I always ask for a helper (as is my right). I then produce a list of products (Darkie toothpaste, Coon cheese from Australia, Robertson's marmalade WITH golly label, etc) only to be told they don't stock them. 'Not even in the ethnic World Foods section?', I enquire politely. 'No, sir' comes the inevitable reply. Draw our own conclusions. – *Relf was Right*

ffs its just a toy 😡 pub geezers just taking the banter to the next level probly never even new its racist? – *bantman*

Precisely! These jolly smiling fellows with their smart bow ties and waistcoats bear no resemblance to the surly menace that stalks our streets. – *Maurice*

We had a coloured girl at my school in Wales in the 1960s and we all called her Golly, even the teachers, and she didn't seem to mind. – *Taffy Meg*

No one is offended except the professionally offended! I remember a time when it was commonplace in the United States of America for lynched corpses and body parts to be displayed in shop windows and sold as souvenirs. Yet no black people ever complained! – *Silent Majority*

I can't wait to see what the radio comedians make of this! They will have a field day! They are like the teachers at school who wore black jeans and made jokes that weren't funny (that wasn't the point) but tried to show that learning was fun! It will make the sheeple who voted Brexit see how stupid they are. It really will. – *Comedy4Progress*

not bein funny but how can golly's be racist if there black? – *Hayley 321*

POETRY CORNER

In Memoriam Ingvar Kamprad, founder of Ikea

So. Farewell
Then Ingvar Kamprad,
Creator of the
"Furniture revolution".

Although, unfortunately,
You were pro-Nazi
In your youth,
You tried to make up
For it by showing
Us all how to build
A better world
(Or, at least a better
Bathroom cabinet or
Shelving unit).

Keith says we are
All trying to put
Together a better world,
But, sadly, we do not all
Have the right Allen key
And often everything
Just falls apart.

E.J. Thribb
(17½ component parts)

In Memoriam Fats Domino

So. Farewell
Then Fats Domino,
King of Boogie-Woogie,
Godfather of
Rock 'n' Roll.

But would you be
Called 'Fats' today?
Or would we
Have to call you
'Differently Sized'
Domino?

Or 'Alternatively
Weighted' Domino?
Or 'Obesity Issues'
Domino?
No, it's not quite
The same.

All together now,
"Ain't That A Shame".

E.J. Thribb (17½ stone)

Ban the Fashion Girls says No one *by Con Voluted*

YES! Time's up for the outdated sexist exploitation of young women forced to sashay up and down the catwalk at fashion industry events.

Why does fashion need to have attractive, semi-naked girls parading around in order to sell its wares?

And spare us the feeble justification that these young women want to do the job and get paid for it, and that banning them will deprive them of their livelihood.

No, the spectacle of glamorous "models" in skimpy outfits pandering to industry moguls must **end** now.

Fashion will just have to attract buyers with the quality of its goods – like any other business!

And while we are at it, surely it's time for attractive young actresses to stop parading around on the red carpet, wearing skimpy outfits in order to flog their films?

This is the 21st century, for heaven's sake, and it really is time for all women to wear burqas or leave public events to men, providing of course that the men are not young, good-looking or wearing skimpy outfits. *(You're fired, Ed.)*

On other pages

Take down all pictures of women ever painted and then put them up again. *(I said you were fired. Ed.)*

"Don't worry – darts will still feature tight tops and large breasts"

Boris Johnson announces bold new building plan

by Our Boris Johnson Announcement Staff
Phil Front-Page

The Foreign Secretary today revealed an exciting new construction scheme which he described as "visionary", "ambitious" and "definitely going to happen, oh yes".

The project, which has been in development since after lunchtime yesterday involves constructing a large Pie in the Sky over Britain.

Said Mr Johnson, "The Pie in the Sky is exactly what this country needs – an infrastructure project which will revitalise British industry and stand as a lasting symbol of British ingenuity and can-do culture."

He continued, "It is a source of some shame that Britain has never been able to construct a vast freestanding aerial pie to hover over the entire country."

The detailed plans on the back of an envelope claim that the advantage of the cloud-level giant savoury pastry project is that it would include a viewing gallery from which the public could survey some other great British landmarks, such as the Boris Channel Bridge, the Boris Garden Bridge over the Thames and the Boris Floating Island Airport in the Thames estuary.

The prime minister, however, said that the foreign secretary's Pie in the Sky idea was unrealistic and was just a manifestation of Mr Johnson's wider plan to construct a future for himself in which his designs on Number 10, Downing Street are realised.

Exclusive to all newspapers

WINE O'CLOCK!
Are baby boomers drinking excessively at home?

by Our Medical Staff **Phil Glass**

According to new research, a whole generation of Britons are putting themselves at risk by opening a bottle as soon as they get home and spending the rest of the evening in an increasingly drunken stupor.

This is, of course, total nonsense. As every journalist knows, people are not beginning their drinking day at home – any self-respecting professional is half-cut by 11am, and really putting it away at lunchtime. By the time they get home, they are merely topping up, which is much healthier.

And another thing, when you think about it, the nanny Shtate could do with a few more of ush booby bamers popping our clogsh, and shortening the NSH waiting lishts. Focush Phil, focush almost time for lunsh. You can do it... Bleeeeuuuurgh!

Nursery Times
········· Friday, Once-upon-a-time ·········

FANTASTIC MR FOX WARNS 'THINGS MAY NOT BE FANTASTIC RIGHT AWAY'

by Our Trade Staff **Baron Hardup**

NURSERYLAND'S Trade Envoy, the Fantastic Mr Fox, returned from meetings with several other countries, including Cloud Cuckoo Land, La La Land, Never Never Land, and China, denying his tail was between his legs.

Said Mr Fox, "I know I told you everything was going to be fantastic at once, but sometimes things don't turn out like fairy tales. There isn't always a happy ending. Sometimes there isn't even a happy beginning. As for the middle – you don't want to know."

Mr Fox continued, "Following discussions with Old Mother Hubbard, it seems that the cupboard isn't entirely full. The Owl and the Pussycat have indicated that they haven't, after all, got plenty of money and have no deal for selling the honey to the inhabitants of the Land Where the Bong Tree Grows.

"But worst of all," added Mr Fox, "this bloody magic lamp I keep rubbing doesn't seem to be responding."

Mr Fox was not available for further comment, but his spokesman, Mr Ferrety Werrity, said, "He's got nothing else to say. Mr Fox has gone to ground."

GLENDA SLAGG

Fleet Street's own spice-filler!?!

■ THE Spice Girls!?!?!! Dontchaluvthem??! Girl power is back and no one is zigazig-happier than this power girl!??!?!?! (Geddit??!) It's music to my ears, the sound of Ginger, Baby, Scary, Sporty and even Posh (!!) belting out those hits of yesteryear!?!! They spice up *my* life!!??!??!! And I wish they could viva forever!!?! I wannabe in the crowd!?? (Geddit??!?) I'll tell you what I want, what I really really want – free tickets!!?!

■ THE Spice Girls!!??!? Arentchasickofthem??!! OK, so they are getting together again in a last-ditch attempt to cash in on their remaining pre-has-been "fame"!??!!! Tell you what, Old Spice, Granny Spice, Wrinkly Spice, Dosh Spice and Greedy Spice!!?!? I'll pay ten million quid not to hear you ever again. I'll tell you what I want, what I really really want – and that's for you to go away!!?!!

■ JOAN Bakewell!!??!! Put a sock in it, Damey!!?! OK, so you had a love romp with theatre's Mr Pause, Harold................. Pinter!!?? (Geddit?? See what I did there??!!) And now you're going to give his love letters to the British Library!!?? Honestly!!?!??! No one wants to read his saucy scribblings, and certainly not the bit about you dressing up as a chambermaid in stockings...!!???! Blimey!!??!!?! It's the British Library, not Stringfellows!!?!

■ HATS off to the Thinking Man's Crumpet!??!! That's Dame Joan Bonkwell to you, Mister!!?! Let's hear it for the frisky bluestocking who's not afraid to show the world her naughty postcards from Horny Harold, aka the Thinking Woman's Crumpy Pumpy!!?! And good to see that the British Library is going to be "The Caretaker" (Geddit??!!) of his notes of "Betrayal" (Geddit??!!) to mark "The Birthday Party" of "The Birthday Party" (Double Geddit!!??)

■ *HERE THEY ARE – Glenda's Erotic Dream Team of Top Tory Totty?!?!*

● **Gavin Williamson**... Mmmm!! He certainly lights my fire!??!! Can I join the "Old Flames", Gavin, as you're clearly smoulderin' hot!?!!

● **Jacob Rees-Mogg** You may be a "weed", but I'd still like to have a scuffle with you!?!?!?!! Mmmm… Moggy!!!????!! I could Eaton you up!?!! (Geddit?!??!!)

● **Ruth Davidson** Hi there, Ruthy!?!! Here's one Scottish sexpot who could make even Auntie Glenda think about swinging to the other side!?!! (Geddit??!!)

Byeee!!

"It's been great being a socialist... but our children are starting school now"

GAVIN WILLIAMSON ADMITS AFFAIR AT FIREPLACE SHOWROOM

Poker?

I've already said I'm not telling you anything else

Jamie's Italian Closing Down Menu In Full

Not-Enough-Doughballs No Breadsticks

Pasta Prima Cannewormzi Meat Ballsup

Inthe Zuppa Inglese Down-the-Pannacotta

– ✳ –

To drink

Bottom of the Barolo Crappa

The Eye's Controversial New Columnist

The columnist who wants a luminous plastic Brexit

This week I am very angry about the judge's harsh words for Julian Assange. Speaking as a baby *(see photo)*, I sympathise with Julian's feelings of imprisonment. I, too, am contained behind bars for the duration. It is both my and Julian's fearless devotion to spreading the truth over the heads of the elite media that is, of course, the real reason why we are persecuted. It is thanks to me that the world now knows that London Bridge is falling down, the ingredients of the device that made that weasel go pop and the identity of the mysterious shadowy figure that supplies "wool" for the little boy who lives down the lane, but the deep state doesn't want you to know these things. That is why I am stuck in this playpen and not because the cat needs an emergency haircut after being covered in Nutella and *(cont. p94)*

"Hey, stop picking on the non-fat kid"

THOSE MAN ILLNESSES EXPLAINED

Man Cold = Well
Man Flu = Cold
Man Aussie Flu = Flu
Man Pneumonia = Aussie Flu
Man at death's door = Pneumonia
Man actually dead = Wife saying
"I thought he was just making it up"

PRESIDENTS CLUB SLEAZE EXPOSED

The Dorchester

It's money for old grope

Exclusive to all papers

- Drunk businessmen groped "hostesses" at City dinner **1-12**
- MPs' "Gropegate" fury **13-15**
- May appoints "Dinner Tsar" **29**
- New laws to curb groping – Rudd will act **36**
- Police investigate dinner gropers **49**
- "My Night of Shame" – dinner "hostess" tells all **76-77**
- "Why oh why?" the nation asks. Your tweets in full **89**
- Shamed Pope admits "I am RC" **94**
- Embarrassed bear confesses to woodland evacuation **95**

(Reuters)

AUCTION REPORT

We are delighted to report the results of the Presidents Club Auction for the right to name a character in the next book by distinguished author David Walliams, who compered the event for five minutes, then left immediately with his head in a bag. The bids were as follows:

- **Mr Alan Oblivious**, a property magnate who loves to leave a party early to go home to spend time with his family, bid £19,000.
- **Sir Michael Outright-Denial**, a business leader who loves spending time with other people's 19-year-old daughters, bid £26,000.
- **Nadhim Zahawi MP** eventually won the auction with a bid of £94,000, for which he apologised and clarified that he hadn't actually meant to bid, he had just put his hand up to call a taxi, as he was outraged by the disgusting behaviour he definitely hadn't seen.

The new book, *Dirty David and the World's Worst Grown-Ups*, will be on sale in October, in no bookshops near you!

---

100 YEARS OF VOTES FOR WOMEN – HOW THINGS HAVE CHANGED

THEN

- Women frequently patronised or given special women's versions of normal products
- Women crowded out of cultural discourse especially when a man is available
- Abuse of women widespread, especially when women speak up about abuse

NOW

- Doritos launching new women-only crisps
- Celebrity Big Brother's women-only edition won by a man
- Women constantly sent death threats on Twitter, especially *(That's enough depressing lack of change. Ed)*

Theresa May 'defiant'

Theresa May struck a defiant tone towards her critics today, as she pledged to remain leader of the Conservative party and Prime Minister right through until the end of this article.

"My message to my detractors is that I am not a quitter and that means remaining leader right through this second paragraph," May told reporters outside Number 10, "and, if necessary, right through until the end of the next paragraph as well. I am in for the long haul."

Cabinet opponents of the Prime Minister, however, insisted it was far-fetched to suggest that May's leadership could last right through to the end of this, the third paragraph, saying her leadership has probably already ended and you still have ten more words left to reach the end of the article.

Awards ceremony just gives out awards

There was widespread shock today after an awards ceremony just gave out awards to actors and musicians and didn't turn itself into a massive political statement about smashing the patriarchy or opposing Donald Trump.

"We just thought we'd give out some awards to actors and musicians and just talk about acting and music," said the awards organiser. "After all, that's what we know about."

However there was an instant backlash on social media, with fans saying they don't want to see their favourite actors and musicians talking about stuff they know about, insisting they should stick to making cringe-worthy speeches about social justice and the rise of fascism – all subjects that had previously escaped their notice – before disappearing off to the green room to get pissed and take a lot of cocaine

'Stop judging me'

The sole surviving suspect from the 2015 Paris terror attacks, Salah Abdeslam, has refused to speak in a Belgian court, saying he will not respond to questions, as Muslims terrorists were "judged mercilessly".

"You take part in one Paris suicide bomb attack, leaving 130 people dead and hundreds more injured, and suddenly you're pigeonholed as being a fundamentalist terrorist," insisted a furious Abdeslam.

"Why are Muslim terrorists like me who take part in these terror attacks singled out in this way and demonised as being terrorists?

"I'd prefer talking about my love of football or my encyclopaedic knowledge of classic '80s movies but no, everyone just harps on and on about my role in this deadly terror attack. Is it any wonder that Muslim terrorists like me feel judged?"

Better get one of each

CARDS
VALENTINE'S DAY
SORRY FOR THE UNWANTED ATTENTION

BOYCE

Faith and Hope distance themselves from Charity

by Our Corinthian Staff
Paul A. Postle

One of the top three virtues in the world of theology faces a backlash following her involvement in a recent scandal.

Charity has been criticised by her colleagues, Faith and Hope,

who have both declared that they are disappointed that she has let herself down and disillusioned all her fans.

Said Hope, "I may spring eternal, but if people stop putting their trust in Charity, then it's going to be me and Faith next."

Added Faith, "If people lose me, then there will be nothing left to believe in."

Charity, once hailed as the greatest of the three, now faces an uphill battle to restore her reputation as the Number One virtue in the religious pantheon.

Already there are rumours that she is to be replaced by the new kid on the virtue-signalling block, Celebrity.

'DON'T GIVE THEM A PENNY' says top columnist PHIL GLASS

OXFAM? Ox-Sham more like! I don't want to say I told you so, but I did. Once again, I've been proved right.

Do-gooders are actually do-badders and most of them are whingeing Left-wing paedophiles who take all your money and spend it on under-age hookers in Roman-style orgies. **Fact.**

Foreign aid never did anyone any good. **Ever.**

Little old ladies in charity shops are wasting their time and, worse than that, are supporting international paedo-gangs who roam the world with impunity, spending the money raised from that moth-eaten cardigan you gave them on champagne, oysters and rent boys. **Double fact.**

It all goes to prove what I've always said. Charity begins at home. But it's better if it doesn't begin at all.

So, next time you hear news of a tragic famine, earthquake or tsunami in some shithole of a country, and the miserable, bearded aid workers shamelessly put out the begging bowl, do yourself and the rest of the world a favour – **go and punch a chugger in the face**.

Burn down your local Oxfam shop. Steal all the money from the collecting tin in the pub. Sue Comic Relief for your money back, even if you didn't give them any.

There's only one way to solve the world's problems. And that's to ignore them. **Ox-Fact**.

PS. Can I have my cheque, please? I'm dying of thirst here.

"Gentlemen, may I introduce to you... my dream team"

The Emperor's New Constitution

by Hans Confucian Andersen

ONCE upon a time there was an Emperor of China who was so powerful that he thought he could do anything he wanted and that everyone would obey him.

So, one day he told his courtiers that he wanted a new, tailor-made constitution that would allow him to rule for ever and ever.

"I wish you to make me Eternal Life President of the People's Empire of China," he said.

And the courtiers went away and made a beautiful new constitution, more beautiful than any the world had ever seen.

And they told Emperor Xi, "We have done as you wished, sire, and you will now live for ever and ever and your kingdom will be the happiest and richest the world has ever known."

And when the Emperor appeared with his new constitution before his people (who had not been consulted on any of this), the crowd all cheered, as they had been told to do.

But one little boy in the crowd stuck up his hand and said, "I'm afraid the Emperor's ambition is completely naked. The new constitution is transparently nonsense."

And when the Emperor heard this, his face went even redder than *The Little Book of Chairman Mao* (lately reissued as *The Even Better Thoughts of Chairman Xi*).

And the Emperor ordered his guards to arrest the little boy and to take him off for a thousand years of re-education in a distant province of the empire.

And peace and harmony were thus returned to the empire.

And all the courtiers marvelled at the perfection of the Emperor's new constitution, saying, "Constitutes you, sire".

And everyone lived happily ever after (except the little boy, obviously).

DIARY

TONY BLAIR

MONDAY: The truth is, these days I'm more "in demand" than ever! I'm, quite literally, rushed off my feet!

I grab breakfast at home, and quickly scan Twitter for reaction to my major keynote speech on the Need for Global Interdependence.

I'm frankly relieved to see that President Trump hasn't tweeted about it!

Nor, incidentally, have my good friends Emmanuel Macron or Angela Merkel, though that's possibly explained by the time difference.

Overall, reaction has been very encouraging. "Excellent speech by Tony Blair on Global Interdependence, worth reading if you have the time," tweets Alastair Campbell, and I'm delighted to say this one's been re-tweeted by independent assessors at the Tony Blair Institute for Global Change. And BBC Wales Today have also retweeted it, which is great. I've said it before, but it's worth saying again: we ignore Wales at our peril.

TUESDAY: Shocked by recent events in Syria, I put an urgent call through to my old buddy President Barack Obama.

"Yo, Barack! Tony here! How's it going? Just keen to touch base over Syria!"

The response is immediate.

"This is the office of President Barack Obama. Please leave your name and the purpose of your call and we will get back to you as soon as possible."

Busy guy, Barack! I only hope I haven't added to his workload through all those media organisations wanting to solicit his response to my latest interventions in the Middle East.

I make a note to self to keep the lines open, because he's bound to ring back the moment he hears who's called.

WEDNESDAY: Find I have a few hours free between a solo working breakfast and perhaps grabbing a bite to eat in the evening, so I go to get a breath of fresh air in the park. You'll never guess who I see walking towards me but my old Cabinet colleagues Peter Mandelson, Harriet Harman and David Blunkett!

I know they're every bit as proud of our achievements in office as I am, so I was thrilled at the opportunity for a bit of a "get-together"! But they clearly hadn't seen me, because as I waved and quickened my step, both Peter and Harriet seemed to dart away.

But at least I could give David a nice surprise! "David! It's Tony!" I said, clapping him on the back.

David seemed genuinely delighted. "Tony!" he said. "I'm genuinely delighted..."

"Brilliant to catch up with you, David. So how's things?"

David turned his wrist towards him. "My goodness!" he said. "Is that the time? Anyway, it was great to have had this little catch-up, Tony! My regards to Cherie!"

Fortunately, as David and his faithful guide dog were striding away – almost running, if I'm being honest! – I spotted Peter and Harriet emerging from behind a tree, so I was pleased to be able to collar them for a chat! "I don't know if you've managed to read my speech to the Kazakhstan Board of Commerce yet," I said.

"Very much in my in-box," said Peter, and Harriet agreed.

"Know what? It feels just like the old days in Cabinet!" I said. "Actually, I was going to get in touch with the two of you about Brexit and its consequences..."

"You'll have to forgive me, Tony. The plumber's due later this afternoon. Or tomorrow. Must rush," said Harriet.

"Oh yes," said Peter. "The plumber! That reminds me! My tap's dripping! See you!"

Respected colleagues, dear friends. Together, we changed things, before things changed.

Memo to self. Dry-cleaning ready for collection Friday a.m.

Barack Obama has still not phoned back. Hope nothing is wrong.

THURSDAY: I'm on great terms with my police protection guys. I like to exchange friendly banter with them as I go in and out of the house.

"Looks like being a nice sunny day!" I said this morning.

"That means it's time to get our umbrellas out," said one to the other.

I guess they misheard what I said!

Still not a peep from Barack, incidentally. I hope I didn't miss the phone ringing while I was watching Countdown.

FRIDAY: I collected the dry-cleaning successfully. The Asian gentleman behind the counter seemed fascinated by what I had to say about the very real threat to democratic accountability from an over-hasty Brexit, but had to break off our conversation when his phone rang.

No word yet from Barack.

Cherie emails to let me know we've just bought an office block in Exeter, a luxury gated development in Costa Rica and a terrace house in Middlesbrough, plus 10,000 acres of prime agricultural land in Southern Romania. Our aim is to make globalisation work for the many, not the few.

On Twitter, there has been a very positive response to yesterday's important tweet from The Tony Blair Institute on the need to reshape national and international priorities. Alastair Campbell has re-tweeted it and so has the influential former head of RBS, Fred Goodwin. The guys at the Institute tell me there's been one helluva lot of media interest too. Looks like a busy weekend ahead of me!

SATURDAY: The guys at the Institute are falling behind! I ask if there's been any word from Andrew Marr or The World at One or Newsnight and they just look blank and say they're working on it.

There's no Countdown on Saturday, so I put a call through to the influential Beverley Turner programme on LBC radio.

"It's Tony from Marylebone. I've got something important to tell Beverley about Syria. And something else about the creation of a new centre-party."

"Putting you through to Beverley now, Tony. Hang on, is that Tony Blair, by any chance?"

"Right first time!"

"Sorry, Tony – we've had a lot of callers today, but do try calling again soon, and thanks for trying!"

Memo to self: try Jeremy Vine on Monday. Or could it be something for You and Yours?

As I leave the house, I tell the guys from my protection squad it's going to be a chilly day. A minute later, I glance back and notice they've removed their jackets.

Still no call from Barack.

As told to

CRAIG BROWN

BRITAIN'S TOP SPIES REVEALED

007

Oh, Oh, Jeremy Corbyn

George Soros is a bit of a funny one, isn't he?

by Our Definitely-Not-Anti-Semitic Correspondent **Nick Timothy**

GEORGE SOROS, the Hungarian billionaire who's been donating money to liberal and anti-Brexit groups, is a bit of a funny one, an exclusive Telegraph investigation has revealed:

1 He's foreign.

2 He doesn't like Brexit.

3 He's part of a global conspiracy of the super-rich… super-rich people devoted to crushing the working man under the yoke of international finance.

4 He's got one of those funny seven-point candle things, what's that all about?

5 You can't get him on the phone on Saturdays.

6 Why won't he eat bacon sandwiches? Eh?

7 If he's such a great guy, why does the reliable Hungarian dictator Viktor Orban dislike him so much?

8 An anagram of Soros' name is "Talmud McShabbat".

9 Er…

10 *(That's enough slightly dubious observations about sinister foreign billionaires. Ed.)*

"There you go"

Jeremy Corbyn
WRITES

HELLO! It's me again. Well, here we go again! Once again, the hated mainstream media is attempting to paint me as some kind of sleeper agent! They're saying I shared information with some communist spy – in a pub of all places!

This is, of course, nonsense. Everyone who knows me knows I do not share information easily – just ask the Labour party! They've been trying to trick information out of me regarding my position on Brexit for months, but they've failed every time! Tough luck, lads! My lips are sealed on that one!

Here is a list of things I've shared in pubs:

1) Beetroot-flavoured organic crisps

2) Badly printed leaflets about Apartheid

3) My favourite joke…
"Knock knock! Who's there? Momentum. Momentum who? Open up, Blairite scum, or we'll put a brick through your window!"

As you can see, it's an extensive list, and sensitive information isn't on there, so let's put those allegations to rest and have no more silly talk about me being a Russian stooge!

What next for the Jihadi Beatles?

IT's the question everyone's asking: Will the Jihadi Beatles reform?

Ever since the news broke of them splitting up after the assassination of Jihadi John, there have been rumours that the remaining members will get together again and try to crack the United States.

That now seems unlikely, as Jihadi George is no longer with us and Jihadi Paul and Jihadi Ringo are both pursuing solo careers in Kurdish prisons.

There are rumours that Jihadi Paul may set up a splinter group of drone operators called Jihadi Wings, or that Jihadi Ringo will provide voiceovers for extremist videos such as "Thomas the Tank".

There are even suggestions that the Bootleg Jihadi Beatles will carry on their work and that their legacy of hits such as "I Want To Cut Off Your Hand" will go on forever.

Meanwhile the Jihadi Stones continue to be thrown at gays and women caught in adultery.

(Paperback Reuters)

Boris Johnson, the Secretary of State for Foreign and Commonwealth Affairs, writes exclusively for Private Eye

CRIPES! Another triumph for Bozza! I've just flown back after sorting out the knotty problem of all those millions of unhappy Rohingya chaps who'd been turfed out of what in happier times we called Burma.

Simple enough. First I spent an hour or two talking to the two million refugees who've been stuck without food or water in Bangladesh, and I could see at once that something needed to be done.

So I beetled off to see the First Lady of what my FO minders keep on telling me I should call Miramar or Miramax, or something like that… Anyway, her name is Aung San Lychee and apparently she is a thoroughly good egg who went to Oxford and won the Nobel Prize for all-round good eggery on human rights, democracy, etc.

I told her in no uncertain terms that she'd better get cracking on taking all those Moslem fellows back into Burma and to make double sure that they got a really warm welcome (and I don't mean the Burmese army burning down their villages again).

The good lady seemed very impressed with what I said, and promised that she would look into the whole thing, and a couple of generals who were standing behind her shook their heads in obvious agreement.

So, job done! Bozza to the rescue again, as when I got those ghastly mullahs to let that poor Iranian woman out of prison (well, nearly).

AN APOLOGY

IN RECENT weeks we have made it very clear, as increasing numbers of women emboldened by the #MeToo movement have come forward to detail sexual harassment, that it is vital that the women making these accusations be believed. When it comes to this issue there can be no mitigating circumstances, and men who use their positions of power to behave inappropriately and force themselves on women deserve nothing but instant vilification and contempt.

We now realise, in the light of women coming forward claiming that Brendan Cox sexually harassed them, that nothing could be further from the truth, that while we accept such behaviour is abhorrent, we need to ask: were there mitigating circumstances which go some way to explaining Brendan's behaviour?

Furthermore, we need to take into consideration how nice he seems, and we need to stress that everyone, certainly people we like, deserve a second chance, especially having come forward without prompting to admit their guilt openly, after just two weekends of front-page exclusives in a Sunday newspaper.

We apologise for any confusion caused, and any confusion in the future, when another Tory minister we don't like is accused of wandering hands and we demand his immediate resignation as, in the #MeToo era, there can be zero tolerance of men who use their powerful position to humiliate and intimidate *(cont. p94)*

AMERICAN SCHOOL SHOOTING SHOCK

by Our Education Correspondent
Sandy Hook

THERE was widespread amazement throughout the United States today, as an entire school managed to reach the end of the day without being massacred by a crazed gunman.

The troubled loner, probably a former classmate, failed to appear at the school at any point and did not begin to shoot indiscriminately with weapons he had recently purchased, despite being known to locals as Mister Nutjob.

Said one stunned pupil, "It was totally unexpected, one minute we were learning math in class and the next minute we still were. How could it not happen?"

A defensive spokesman for the National Rifle Association, Mr Lou Scannon, said, "If only more people had been armed then this wouldn't have happened."

He was supported by the President of the United States, who tweeted: "My thoughts and prayers go out to all those who haven't been murdered in their classrooms today. Good luck tomorrow. #learn-nothing".

ASSAULT RIFLE... ...WITH SILENCER

Revolution in film industry as it emerges black superheroes can be incredibly boring too

by Our Comic Staff **Andrew Marvell**

THE new film *Black Panther*, about a black superhero battling to save a fictional African country, has united critics on one point: for the first time, the industry is waking up to the fact that it's now possible to have an overlong, tiresome movie stuffed with unnecessary special effects *even with hardly any white people in it*!

"This is a massive step forward," said one producer. "For years we were under the impression that we had to keep making boring, CGI-stuffed juggernauts featuring only white people, one or two tokenistic parts aside. It now turns out that we can keep on making the same crappy superhero films as before, with a completely black cast, and be hailed as absolute geniuses for it. It's a game-changer."

Another added, "We thought we were clever when last year we made Wonder Woman and realised female superheroes can be tiresomely perfect too, but this is even better."

"The huge critical success of *Black Panther* has opened a new chapter of film-making," said a third. "From now on, you're going to have to endure hours of arse-numbing fight scenes with a greater representation of ethnic minority on screen, and afterwards, when you leave the cinema complaining about the complete lack of character depth, the characters who will have that lack of depth may very well be black."

Marvel confirmed that as well as *Black Thor*, *Black Guardians of the Galaxy* and *Black Avengers*, they are now working on the next 94 *Black Panther* sequels, in which *(That's enough Marvel films of any colour. Ed.)*

THINGS THAT STOP A BAD GUY WITH A GUN

1 A good guy with a gun

2 A systematic programme to stop bad guys, and in fact most guys, from getting their hands on incredibly powerful guns in the first place

3 A thoughts and prayers dispenser to be fitted in all school restrooms *(You're fired, Ed.)*

DAVIDSON BACKS LEADER

We should all unite behind a strong woman

Human history

ME TOO.

Lookalikes

Lion   **Cumberbatch**

Sir,
When I bumped into Benedict Cumberbatch in the gardens of a stately home recently, I was struck by how much he reminded me of something. I now realise that he is the image of the lion that appeared frequently in the last series of Sherlock. Is Wanda Ventham perhaps the cat's mother?
LUCY QUINNELL.

Nick Clegg   **Waiter**

Sir,
Has anyone noticed the resemblance between Chaim Soutine's portrait of a waiter contemplating his past mistakes, bad decisions and missed opportunities, and Nick Clegg. Maybe a knighthood would cheer him up?
ROB KELLY.

Julia Hartley-Brewer   **Nurse Ratched**

Sir,
I believe Nurse Ratched from "One Flew Over The Cuckoo's Nest" had a rather conservative outlook on the world, as does Julia Hartley-Brewer.
JOHN FINAGIN,
S.E. London.

Quentin Letts   **Thomas**

Sir,
Bubbling boilers! Has anyone spotted the similarity between the cheeky little tank engine from Sodor, Thomas, and the Brexit-cheerleading Daily Mail columnist, Quentin Letts? Could they be perhaps related?
BRIAN JENNER.

Ron Mael   **Prince Albert**

Sir,
Imagine my surprise when the gripping historical realism of ITV's Victoria was sullied by our greatest monarch marrying the keyboard player from Sparks.
STEVE BALDOCK,
Handcross, W. Sussex.

The Joker   **Catherine Deneuve**

Sir,
A remarkable air de famille strikes me between the joker whom I've seen on TV opposing the forces of righteous justice and the villain played by Cesar Romero.
ALUN MORRIS,
Cottenham.

Droopy   **Ant**

Sir,
Is it at all possible that Droopy the Dog and Ant Whatever are related? They both have smaller on-screen partners and manage to win out in the end, despite the odds being drawn against them.
TERRY McCRUM.

David Davis   **Private Godfrey**

Sir,
I wonder if your readers have noticed the uncanny resemblance of two old soldiers, Private Godfrey, who modestly concealed his heroics as a medical orderly in WW2, and David Davis, with his much-vaunted experience as a part-time SAS reservist some time back in the last millennium. Might Godfrey, bearing a conciliatory plate of Dolly's cucumber sandwiches, get us a better deal in Brussels?
DON T. LIKET-UPHAM.

Man in the Moon   **Sajid Javid**

Sir,
Is the new Home Secretary the man in the moon?
JOHN LAMBERT.

Knock   **Vince Cable**

Sir,
It occurred to me during a recent evening of TV horror, that the Rt Hon Sir Vince Cable MP bears an uncanny resemblance to the insane and delusional character Knock from Murnau's 1922 silent classic, 'Nosferatu'.
MR CHRISTOPHER WILSON.

Borg Cube   **US Embassy**

Sir,
Surely I cannot be alone in noticing the resemblance between the new American embassy in London, and a Borg Cube? One represents one of the greatest threats to peace and stability in the galaxy. The other is from the television programme "Star Trek".
PHILIP BROCKLEHURST,
Twickenham.

Dracula   **Mary Trump**

Sir,
This could go a long way to explaining the behaviour of her son – it's well known that Mary Trump and Dracula were never seen in the same room at the same time.
ROB COOKSON.

Potato head   **Rupert Murdoch**

Sir,
Has anyone noticed, as I have, the extraordinary resemblance between the executive chairman of News Corp and 21st Century Fox and this potato?
ENA B. EDWARDS.

THE TIMES OF LONDON

FEBRUARY 23RD 1936

Olympic Cheerleaders Delight World

by Our Sports Staff **E. Zilly-Deupt**

It's the image that is lighting up the Olympics, as thousands of supporters for the regime that's come in from the cold show their appreciation for their athletes, their nation and their leader.

Crowds have really enjoyed the spectacle of all those immaculately synchronised youngsters, in matching brown shirts and swastika armbands, raising their right arms and their voices to the sky, to chant "Heil Hitler" and sing the delightful folk-song "Tomorrow Belongs to Me".

So much for the nay-sayers who thought it was a bad idea to have an Olympics in Germany and that Mr Hitler would in some way hijack the event for his own propaganda purposes.

No, these "Peace Olympics" will go down in history as the moment when fears of a global conflict could be put to one side and we could enjoy the simple pleasures of blond, blue-eyed youngsters displaying their devotion to an unstable and murderous despot.

Said one BBC correspondent, "Thank heavens they've brought some much needed colour to our coverage – there's a limit to how many times we can watch a British competitor falling over and disappointing everyone."

On other pages

■ Hitler consort Ms Braun brings ray of sunshine to chilly Berlin Games **p5**

■ Another British competitor falls over **p17**

■ World War II declared **p94**

Britain 'convincingly feigns interest in curling'

BRITAIN has once again, as is the case every four years during the Winter Olympics, been gripped by "feigning interest in curling" fever.

"It's every bit as gripping and utterly edge-of-your-seat stuff as everyone says," said Karen of Hemel Hempstead. "I only fell asleep twice on the sofa earlier watching it."

"Forget Usain Bolt and Mo Farah, for getting the pulse racing there's nothing quite like lawn bowls on ice crossed with street sweeping," said Andy of Cirencester (*cont. 2022, 2026, 2094, etc*)

POETRY CORNER

**In Memoriam
Charles Lazarus, founder
of Toys Я Us, who died
just one week after his
company folded**

So. Farewell
Then Charles Lazarus,
Or should that be
Laz Я Us?

Sadly, like your
Company, you Я
No more.

And, unlike your
Biblical namesake,
Lazarus, you Я not
Coming back.

ЯIP.

E.J. Thribb
(17½ batteries not included)

*"No doubt they'll be
taking the company
car back"*

Why oh why do they have to stage the Winter Olympics in a country that's so cold? asks Phil Freezer

THERE'S only one question on everyone's frozen lips here, as they stand around shivering or huddle together for warmth, trying to watch these chillingly cold Winter Olympics in PyeongChang: Why was the International Olympic Committee crazy enough to think of holding winter games in a country that is covered in snow and ice and where the temperatures plummet below freezing point?

Why couldn't they be sensible enough to hold them in a country like Chad or Qatar?

Pictures with New Titles, No.1

Napoleon Tries to Remember Where He Parked His Car,
Vereshchagin 1887-95

HOW TO KEEP WARM IN COLD WEATHER

■ Buy newspaper full of boring stories about the snow

■ Burn newspaper

■ Hey presto – you're warm

Those names for the next storm in full

Storm Emma

Storm Sense and Sensibility

Storm Stormzy

Storm Jacob Rees-Fogg

Storm Teacup

Storm Trooper

Storm Ont (Northern Ireland only)

Storm N. Norman (Iraq only)

British Home Storm

Storm Snowy McSnowface

Trains cancelled due to money on line

LARGE numbers of trains throughout Britain were cancelled today due to the availability of financial compensation for operators if they just gave up and cancelled all the trains at the news of the first snowflake heading across the Urals.

BBC NEWS

White hell misery as Britain groans under winter disaster. Entire country falls apart and everyone deeply unhappy.

"Miss Penny, the children need to go home early first"

DAILY ⊕ EXPRESS

FRIDAY MARCH 9, 2018

BRITAIN BROUGHT TO STANDSTILL BY 'BLIZZARD OF THE CENTURY'

by Our Weather Staff
Will Wright-Anything

THERE was widespread astonishment in the office of *The Daily Express* today when one of its regular front-page stories actually came true, as snow did in fact have Britain in its icy grip.

"We just write this 'storm of the century' guff every other week," said one bemused hack, "we never actually expect it to happen!"

Following this unprecedented event, there was much speculation that every *Daily Express* headline would come true eventually.

"We're looking forward to the miracle seaweed pill really being the cure for arthritis and eating dark chocolate actually preventing dementia," said one media onlooker. "Not to mention there being an actual, real breakthrough in the search for Madeleine McCann.

"I'm sure when the ghost of Princess Diana appears outside Kensington Palace she'll be delighted to find out that everything in the Daily Express is true. It really is."

Daily Mail, Friday, March 9, 2018

The Mail Says

FOREIGN WEATHER SHOULD GO HOME!

IT'S time that Britain took back control of its own weather and stopped foreign snowstorms pouring across our borders and dictating how we run our country.

Railways, motorways, schools, airports, offices have all been brought to a grinding halt by having to follow the diktats of continental weather patterns.

We say enough is enough. It's time that we told the unelected pressure systems and unaccountable cloud formations of other continents to stay out of Britain and leave us to decide on our own weather which, if it was up to us, would be sunny, temperate and agreeable, rather than the compulsory white hell, as stipulated by the *(This is mad. More, please. Paul Dacre)*

On other pages

● Has Siberian storm been orchestrated by Jeremy Corbyn on instructions from his Russian paymasters? *(No.)*

EveningStandard

Friday 9 March 2018

SNOW CHAOS ENTIRELY FAULT OF THERESA MAY

by Our **Entire Staff**

AS BRITAIN suffered the worst snow storm in history, experts were unanimous in pointing the finger of blame at the Prime Minister.

"She's snow use at all," said one meteorologist whom we've made up, and… *(Cont. pages* **2-94**)

Morning Tsar

VLAD THE IMPALER DENIES IMPALING ANYONE

by Our Terror Staff
Martin Ivans The Terrible

AFTER a number of suspicious deaths involving people impaled on stakes, the finger of suspicion has been pointed at Vladimir "The Putin" Impaler.

The Eastern European strong man, famous for parading around without his tunic on, yesterday denied that the deaths had anything whatsoever to do with him: "Admittedly, they were all my enemies and I had vowed vengeance on them, but people are just taking two and two and making four."

When asked by investigative scribes about the stakes which contained the legend: "If found please return to V. Impaler", Mr Impaler looked extremely affronted.

"Send me these stakes and I will do an independent analysis as to their provenance, which will find that I have never clapped eyes on these stakes of mine before."

He went on, "Are you questioning me? Because I still have lots of stakes, which you might inadvertently fall on top of".

To which the reply was, "Absolutely not. I now realise, sir, that all these people stole the stakes and deliberately impaled themselves in order to try to make you look bad.

"Congratulations on your election victory next week!"

It's Police Constable country

ITALIAN RESTAURANT REOPENS

I'd avoid the Putinesca

Notes&queries

What is Novichok?

● Novichok, writes **Professor Simon Sarin**, as the name suggests, is a brand of "novelty chocolate" bar made out of 85% cocoa-style fat substitutes and hugely popular in Mexico where the branding features a cartoon sloth called "Zappy" who wears a sombrero. According to Zappy, eating Novichok gives him a huge energy boost between meals, although the World Health Organisation has specifically denied these claims and warned that Novichok can lead to obesity, diabetes and premature death.

● Professor Sarin's research is sadly faulty, writes **Dr Clemmie Chlorine**, as a rudimentary glance at the recent results in the Wimbledon Ladies Championship would have confirmed. Natalia Novichok is the Uzbekistan No.3, who nearly took a game off Serena Williams in the second set of her Round 2 encounter with the American multiple-grand-slam victor on Court 94 in 2015. The final score (6-0, 6-0) did not do justice to the fine efforts of the plucky Uzbeki left-hander with the deadly serve who I am sure will one day surprise us all as a giant-killer here in Britain.

● The good doctor really needs her eyes tested, says **Reverend Millie Mustard**. Whilst on a recent ecumenical conference in Leighton Buzzard, I had the pleasure of staying in one of the Novichok motels on the roundabout by the slip road leading to the A1735. These modern "no frills, no breakfast, no room" motels offer you the chance to sleep in your own car whilst parked in a secure car park. They are clean, functional and cheap, and an ingenious use of formerly toxic brownfield contamination sites. What better way to wake up refreshed and ready to do battle over the thorny issue of transsexual bishops who want to identify as Methodists?!

Answers please:
Is Lady Judge a Judge?
Who are the Fisher People?

GOVERNMENT ADVICE IN FULL

To British residents of Salisbury...

Launder Your Clothes

To Russian oligarchs in London...

Launder Your Money

"Am I the homeowner? Of course not, I'm only forty-five"

COUNTDOWN TO BREXIT

Ten, nine, eight, seven... then a transition period... seven, six, five, then renegotiation... five, six, seven... then...

GNOMEMART
PRODUCT RECALL

The Brexit Advent Calendar, which counted down the days to our departure from the EU on 29 March 2019, has had to be withdrawn due to an unforeseen complication. The calendar originally featured 365 windows, which you closed one by one, depriving yourself of specific goods, viz a Belgian chocolate on one day, a glass of Italian Prosecco the next, a German-made car the day after, and so on. Due to the introduction of an additional 21-month transition period, a further 640 windows now need to be added. If you bought one of the original calendars, simply send it back and wait for your replacement. **Warning**: new calendar now measures 94 square feet and may not fit through your letterbox.

Get your Great British Calendar now! Made in France.

THE LABOUR PARTY
An Apology

IN RECENT years, we in the Labour Party may have given the impression that the Party was in no way anti-Semitic or hostile to persons of the Jewish faith. We even commissioned the highly respected Labour peer, Lady Shami Chakrabarti, to produce a comprehensive report wholly clearing the party of being guilty of any such vile and unacceptable prejudices.

We now realise, in light of various unfortunate incidents which have received rather embarrassing publicity in the media, that the Labour Party does indeed contain pockets of anti-Semitism and has a significant number of members whose views on those of Jewish ethnicity are at best inappropriate and, at worst, could lose us the next election.

We would like to express our profound apologies for any offence this may have caused, and firmly pledge that in future we will do absolutely nothing about it.

©*The Labour Party (J. Corbyn prop.)*

"These mice are smarter than we think – it's a trompe l'oeil!"

PRINCE WILLIAM WITHDRAWN FROM WORLD CUP

by Our Football and Chemical Weapons Correspondent **Nobby Chok**

AFTER the flagrant breach of sovereignty by Vladimir Putin's despotic regime, the prime minister, Theresa May, has shown her strength as a world leader and followed through with her threat to retaliate in the toughest manner possible, issuing the following statement:

"We could have frozen the assets of Russian oligarchs. We could have launched a cyber attack against Russian installations. But no, we have gone far further. We have politely asked Prince William if, rather than make the most of some free tickets, he would deign to watch the football on telly instead."

The news has stunned the whole of Russia. An openly weeping Vladimir Putin said, "Having bribed our way into hosting this competition, we thought we could do whatever we liked. But we weren't expecting this level of backlash."

Battle of Wills

Through tears of laughter he added, "I have no idea what we'll do, probably give his seats to some deserving Russian hero. Like the bloke who did the poisoning in the first place. Though I wouldn't sit next to him if I were you."

BORIS ATTACKS VOTE-RIGGING CLAIMS

To suggest that Leave won through dirty tricks...

...is a lie

Whistleblower 'outed'

by Our Investigative Reporter
Dai Vulge

THERE was fury at Westminster after a gay whistleblower was intentionally outed by Downing Street as a former Vote Leave staffer.

"I've endured the worst 48 hours of my life," the gay whistleblower told reporters.

"Within the London homosexual community there is a huge amount of prejudice against those admitting they're a Leave campaigner. Most prefer to hide away that aspect of their life and not discuss it publicly, for fear of being ostracised from the gay community.

"Coming out as being in favour of coming out of the EU is just not seen as something which is socially acceptable in the cloistered world of trendy Shoreditch cafes and themed gay bars."

FACEBOOK HARVESTED DATA FROM MILLIONS OF PEOPLE

THERE was shock around the world yesterday as it emerged that a tax-dodging, secretive, social media website run by a megalomaniac billionaire turned out not to be very nice.

ON OTHER PAGES
- Pope Harvested Souls For Catholic Church
- Bear Harvested Toilet Paper For Trip to Woods

HIDDEN DANGERS

| **Iceberg** | **Fatberg** | **Zuckerberg** |

---

life hacks

How to keep your personal data secure on Facebook

1. Delete your Facebook account

2. Go outside, take a walk... enjoy the fresh air... pop into the pub... chat to people

3. Er...

4. That's it.

"Oh my God! Making my entire life public has robbed me of my privacy!!"

Sarah Vain

#MeMeMeMeToo!!

THE politically correct brigade would have us walking on eggshells around the sensitive topic of the moment – Fatuous Shaming.

But let me tell you, I was fatuous-shamed and it did me a power of good.

Yes, it was humiliating to be told bluntly, "You're fatuous", but you know, when I looked in the Mirror, or rather the Mail, I thought, "Yes, I am fatuous and, more importantly, I can get another column out of it!"

So here it is. It's the new, slimmed down, lightweight Sarah Vain column.

Thin stuff, eh, readers?

WHY ARE YOU SO SENSITIVE ABOUT YOUR FEELINGS?

THAT IS A VERY HURTFUL QUESTION!

The Tortoise and the David Hare

New BBC state-of-the-nation drama

(Enter lovable, sympathetic, mysterious tortoise)

Tortoise *(talking to self in mirror)*: I'm a lovable, sympathetic, mysterious tortoise, remember?

(Enter moody, irascible, arrogant hare)

Hare: Hi Tortoise, I'm a moody, irascible, arrogant Hare, what are you doing here in Tory Britain, you old tortoise, you?

Tortoise: Speaking as a tortoise, which I am, one thing I'm not going to do is challenge you to a race, because, as you remember, I'm a tortoise and I have a back-story of being quite slow.

Hare: Well this is Thatcher's Britain and you, Tortoise, own your own home.

Tortoise: By which you mean the shell on my back, I suppose. Because I'm a tortoise, remember?

Hare: Let's get this race that I'm going to win over with because in Cameron's posh-boy Britain there are only winners and no time for losers. That's why race is a very big issue in today's society.

Tortoise: As is gender politics. I'm a lesbian, remember?

Hare: Oh yes, and I'm an illegal immigrant. What are you doing with that gun? Are you going to start this race?

Tortoise: No, I'm going to become a serial killer, because I'm suffering from Post Traumatic Stress Disorder, having served in Iraq in one of Tony Bliar's illegal wars supporting the American military industrial complex.

Hare: Oh yes, I remember. As you probably remember that as well as being an illegal immigrant, I'm a former pole-vaulter who became a detective.

Tortoise: That makes sense to me. So when do we get to do this race?

Hare: Not till episode four.

(All viewers go to sleep along with Hare. Thus allowing Tortoise to win race – spoiler alert!)

YES, IT'S FUCK NEWS!

THEN

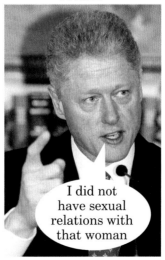

I did not have sexual relations with that woman

NOW

I did not have sexual relations with that woman... or that one... no, not that one either...

47

THE AUSTRALIAN
EDITORIAL

The ball-tampering scandal that has brought shame to a great cricketing nation

FAIR DINKUM. Two words which capture the spirit and essence of our national Australian character. As a country, we pride ourselves on the noble concept of Dinkum.

Dinkum runs through our veins, our DNA, and our very souls. Without Dinkum, what are we? Without Dinkum, who are we? Without Dinkum, why are we? Without Dinkum we are no further up the evolutionary scale than a rabid wombat.

And yet, in one moment of madness, one rub of soiled yellow sticky tape on a leather cricket ball, our cherished Dinkum has been brought into disrepute. Traduced, denigrated, besmirched, our beloved Dinkum is Fair no more!

Action must be taken at the highest levels. There is only one way to restore Dinkum, our national pride, and our sense of ourselves.

Yes, let's crack open a shitload of tinnies and neck 'em till we chunder.

Old-fashioned Australian ball tampering

BALLOT TAMPERING SCANDAL LATEST

"We didn't cheat. We won fair and square. Everyone else does it anyway. What's the problem? Suck it up, losers!"

THOSE AUSTRALIAN FIELDING POSITIONS IN FULL

- First Slip
- Second Blunder
- Third Cock-Up
- Silly Mid On
- Bloody Silly Mid On
- Sticky Wicket Keeper
- Sticky Tape Keeper
- Extra Cover-Up
- Hefty Fine Leg
- Deep DooDoo

DID AUSSIES CHEAT IN THE ASHES?

Comic Relief to ban 'white donors'

by Our Aid Staff
Achroma Topsia

The charity Comic Relief has indicated that in its bid to move on from "white saviour" stereotyping it will not only scrap white celebrities like Eddie Redmayne and Ed Sheeran from fronting its films about African poverty, but will also ban white people from giving money to the charity.

Said chief executive Ms Trigger Warner, "The idea that desperate people in developing countries need saving from famine and disease by the intervention of so-called charities from western nations, predominantly full of white people, is extremely offensive."

Ms Warner continued, "Haven't we had enough of oppressive colonialist racism in the west without encouraging people in countries like Britain to think that Africa is full of desperate black people who need their help?

"It is a disgrace that this charity even exists, even more disgraceful that I, as a white person, am the chief executive and totally disgraceful that anyone should give us any money and... er... *(not continued for long)*

Those Hugh Grant Rom-Coms In Full

- Five Children and No Weddings
- Love Child Actually
- Bachelor Paddington

- Bachelor Paddington 2
- Nine Months (1,2,3,4,5)
- Tie A Notting Hill In It!
  (I said, that's enough films. Ed)

GLENDA SLAGG

The Beast from the Street!! (Geddit??!!)

■ YES!!! It's official!! They're bigger than the Beatles!! It's the royal Fab Four I'm talkin' about, Mister!!! Wills, Kate, Harry and Meghan are the new John, Paul, George and Ringo!!? And they're all singin' in perfect harmony and makin' beautiful music!?!! With lead singer Meghan, they're provin' that All You Need Is Love and consigning pub rockers Chaz 'n' Cam to the dustbin of pop history!!?! (Geddit??!!)

■ FAB FOUR??!! Don't make me laugh!!? There's only one similarity to the Beatles and that's the foreign one who comes in, marries the star and then splits them all up, ie Meghan Ono aka Yoko!??! With her hippy-dippy, touchy-feely, huggy-muggy New Age claptrap, Meghan spells disaster for the most successful British group in history!?! All together now, "Help!!!"

■ CIVILISATIONS!? Dontcha-luvit?? OK, I haven't watched it, but who cares??! Good to see all the high-falutin' artsy fartz brigade putting the boot into each other??!! Gompertz vs Beard!!?!? Marr vs Schama!!?!!? Sour vs Grapes??!!? Talk about uncivilised!!? (Geddit??!)

■ TALKING about ancient relics, have you seen the nooz about the Rolling Stones??!! They're going on a world tour!!? Really, Grandad!?? Where??? Eastbourne, Worthing, Frinton, Bournemouth and then a grand finale in the Dignitas clinic in Switzerland??!! Give it a rest, old timers, and stick to what you're good at, ie slagging each other off in the papers for being too old to have children!!??!

■ HATS off to the Rolling Stones!?! OK, so they've been around longer than Stonehenge, but they've still got what it takes to make this gal throw her M&S knickers (with the seam on the side!!?) at Jumpin' Jack Jagger!!?? Mmmm!!! Come on Keith, Mick, Ron and Charlie, aka the Fab Four!!?! We still love you even though you're 64, or is it 84?!?!

(That's the Beatles. You're fired. Ed.)

Byeee!!

How does one become a millionaire?

A: Become a nurse

B: Become a charity worker

C: Become a teacher

D: Punch a producer and clear off to Amazon

"Want to bet how many betting ads they can fit into the break?"

The Eye's Controversial New Columnist

The columnist whose bedroom is the subject of a Disney takeover

This week I am very angry at the derision aimed at Mark Rylance for his views on Shakespeare. Mr Rylance, like myself, is a renowned opinion-holder who is not afraid to put forward his opinions in a fruity, authoritative-sounding way. In that light, I am happy to correct a controversy that has agitated literary scholars for years. Did Roger Hargreaves write the "Mr Men" books? Even though I did not know Mr Hargreaves, or his family, or have studied a great deal on the subject, the fact that I am speaking as a baby (*see photo*) and have had them read to me, means that I am an expert on them and my word is the last word on the matter.

The answer is "no". Roger Hargreaves could not have written the "Mr Men" books. This is because he was just an ordinary man, and not a duke or a Cambridge professor, and he could not have experienced the huge range of emotions that the Mr Men have. There is no way he could have been uppity AND mean AND happy AND slow AND rushy AND lazy AND busy! There is no way he could have used his imagination to think himself into the mind of Mr Bump. That would be unprecedented in the history of human fiction-writing.

---

facebook QUIZ

WHAT SORT OF MUPPET ARE YOU?

Question 1.

Are you still doing Facebook quizzes even after the revelations that doing these quizzes is how you enable companies such as Cambridge Analytica to mine your personal data online to build up a comprehensive psychological profile of you for marketing purposes? Yes ○ No ○

If you answered yes –
CONGRATULATIONS! YOU ARE SWEETUMS.
That is the biggest and stupidest muppet in the muppet world.

SPICE GIRLS TO GO TO ROYAL WEDDING

Ginger   **Scary**

Sporty

Baby

Posh

MOGG ATTACKS 'CRETINOUS' GOVERNMENT

by Our Brexit Staff **Cliff Edge**

TORY backbench superstar, Jacob Rees-Fogg, heir to the Phileas Fogg round-the-world snacks empire, last night launched a devastating attack on the government, which he said he "thoroughly supports".

Fogg, known for his impeccable manners and unfailing courtesy, described Theresa May as a "useless cretin" for suggesting that we should continue trading with the EU in any way at all.

Fogg called for "hard borders" to keep out what he called "those dreadful foreigners", along with all their "ghastly ships, horrid trains and smelly lorries full of their awful goods".

He continued, "Why have we wasted over a year talking to these recalcitrant continentals, when the obvious answer is simply to walk out and have nothing to do with Europe ever again?

"We should go back to the good old days, when we only needed to trade with our friends in the Empire or, as I believe it's now called in politically-correct Metropolitan elite circles, the Commonwealth."

Mr Fogg declared that "We would be perfectly content buying and selling with such splendid little countries as St Kitts, Tristan de Cunha and the Gilbert and Sullivan Islands, now unfortunately known, I gather, as Kiritekanawa and Metoovalu.

"People go drearily on about these silly trade terms. When it comes to Great Britain buying and selling with places like the Caicos and Eatos Islands, all that matters is that they do the buying and we do the selling."

When critics last night pointed out that all Mr Fogg's money came from an international business, trading around the entire world in eighty days, the crisps-to-private-equity-fund millionaire joked, "You're all a bunch of cretins or, as we Latin speakers say, *cretinuses cretinorum*."

THE WISDOM OF SOLOMON

OK, now sort out the dispute over the Northern Ireland border

I quit

'90 percent of Brexit now agreed' says upbeat Davis

by Our Brexit Staff **Cliff Edge**

A triumphant Brexit secretary, David Davis, yesterday told a packed Brussels conference, "We're almost there with our negotiations. We're on the brink of a brilliant deal that's win-win for everyone."

With a broad smile, Mr Davis assured his audience that "we are now in total agreement on 90 percent of the issues".

When asked to confirm the 10 percent of subjects that still had to be resolved, Mr Davis looked momentarily nonplussed until a helpful official handed him an A4 sheet of paper.

Putting on his glasses, Mr Davis peered at the sheet with an apparent look of surprise and began reading.

"Issues outstanding: Irish border, terms of future trade deal with EU, terms of future agriculture deal with EU, terms of future fisheries deal with EU, future of defence cooperation, security links, foreign policy, chemicals, medicines, aviation, including air traffic control, how to keep British ports open, the survival of the City of London, er…"

At this point, Mr Davis stopped reading and suggested that going into too much detail was not very helpful and that it was probably time for everyone to go off to have lunch.

TV star addiction shock

by Our Painkiller Addiction Staff **Anna Din** and **Barry Cetamol**

IT WAS a tragedy unfolding before our eyes. At first, it was just once a week "for a bit of fun", but all too soon it spiralled into a full-blown three-times-a-week dependency, which left ITV desperately vulnerable.

When the crunch came, the broadcaster's addiction to Ant and Dec was laid bare for all to see. They literally couldn't cope without them. Said ITV boss, Kevin Lygo, "I thought I could handle it. I thought I could kick the Ant and Dec habit any time I

wanted to. But you get to Saturday evening and you suddenly have a craving you can't control and, before you know it, you've got a multi-million-pound habit."

He continued, "I'm no stranger to highs and lows, but the low ratings we're facing are truly terrifying. I've tried going full turkey (*The Nightly Show* with David Walliams), but it didn't work – it just left me and the handful of viewers really depressed. Soon I was back on the Ant and Dec."

ITV have announced that they're going into rehab – to film Ant if at all possible.

Who do you think should replace Mr Anthony McPartlin in the top shiny-floor reality jungle entertainment double act of all time?

Ann and Dec

Anton and Dec

Lady Ant and Dec

Adam Ant and Dec

Antigone and Dec

Rembrandt and Dec

MILITARY STRIKE 'A RESOUNDING SUCCESS'

by Our Over-excited War Correspondent **Tom Cruise Missile**

THE Prime Minister announced that the Syrian air strike had dramatically achieved its primary objective.

Speaking to a press conference, Theresa May congratulated herself for a limited, proportional, but highly effective attack on the designated target, namely Jeremy Corbyn.

"Corbyn has been degraded and his ability to strike back has been seriously compromised," she declared.

"We won't be hearing from him again and it's game over for him."

The Prime Minister gave further details of the operation, which involved the launch of a so-called "Spart bomb", which was extraordinarily effective in neutralising extreme Left-wing opponents.

"What the Spart bomb has done is to leave Corbyn saying that we should have got UN approval when he knows that Russia vetoed it."

Mrs May continued, "The Spart bomb is cleverly designed to confuse Corbyn until he blows up and shouts that it was nothing to do with Russia anyway."

Asked by reporters whether any other objectives had been achieved by the raid, she pointed to the fact that not one journalist had brought up the subject of Brexit.

Concluding her press conference, the Prime Minister praised the joint action, saying, "This goes to show what can be achieved if Britain and her ally France stick together and... er... no more questions."

SYRIAN BOMBING

'I WATCH OUR BOYS GO IN'

An eye witness account by
Features Writer of the Year (1997) Phil Space

IT WAS 3.37am and dawn was just coming up over the hillside when I saw with my own eyes a text message from my editor on my mobile. *"Turn on Sky News"* it said bluntly and so I did.

What happened next was incredible. I stumbled downstairs, made myself a cup of coffee and switched on the television.

There, amazing scenes greeted my eyes. It was *Friends*, the one they always repeat, but there was no time for life's ordinary pleasures.

6,000 miles away in Syria, Sky News was showing missiles being fired, bombs dropping, chemical installations blowing up and Ray Winston telling me to put a bet on Stoke v Sunderland.

I could scarcely believe it and the speed of events took me by surprise.

Within seconds my editor had texted again: *"Where's that fucking 1,000-word piece?"* And from then on, everything was panic, confusion, noise and chaos, as I unleashed the dogs to go outside and do their business while I wrote some desperate guff about war on the telly.

Then suddenly, it was over. Or was it? Another message from my editor read coldly: *"This is bollocks. Put in some stuff about celebrities' response on Twitter".*

Never had the old adage been truer "War is Hello". *(You're fired. Ed).*

On other pages

● Graphic artists mobilise in largest display ever seen of cut-aways of aircraft and ships, mocks-ups of explosions and locator maps with enormous big black arrows on them.

"Didn't you liberate us last year?"

What was the top secret Allied bombing operation of Syria actually called?

- ▨ Operation Stable Door
- ▨ Operation Empty Gesture
- ▨ Operation Knee Jerk
- ▨ Operation Here We Go Again
- ▨ Operation Fingers Crossed
- ▨ Operation Don't Rock The Boat
- ▨ Operation Savey McSaveFace
- ▨ Operation Will This Do?
- ▨ Operation Desert Stormy Daniels

(That's enough stupid names. Ed)

SMART MISSILE

THIS IS STUPID.

A Doctor Writes

Alfie's Syndrome

AS A doctor, I'm often asked, "Are you a murderer?" The simple answer is "I'm calling the police".

What happens in these cases is that initially the medical practitioner is faced with an ethical dilemma which he or she seeks to address using scientific evidence, humanitarian judgement and informed reason.

What then follows is that the doctor becomes a victim of those suffering from *sentimentalis humbuggeris religiosis fundamentalis* or Alfie's Syndrome, as it is known colloquially.

Symptoms of this distressing condition include threatening to burn down children's hospitals and to commit violence against medical staff, and carrying banners proclaiming you are pro-life whilst threatening to kill people. There is no known cure for victims of Alfie's Syndrome and even death does not stop the virulence and toxicity of the affliction.

If you are worried about being called a murderer, so am I.

© *A. Doctor 2018*

Should Nigel Farage be allowed home to die?

by Our Medical Correspondent
Neo Natal

THERE were increasing calls today, after Nigel Farage's repeated appearances on Fox News talking total nonsense about the Alfie Evans case, for the former Ukip leader to be allowed to go home where his credibility can die in peace.

"Watching Farage give credence to far-right US propaganda about NHS death panels proves there is no discernible brain activity there any more," said a spokesman for the medical staff at Alder Hey hospital.

"We agree that it would be inhumane to prolong the suffering of the British public any further, so the time has come to withdraw Farage from the airwaves and send him home."

The landlord of the Dog & Duck confirmed that he would be happy to look after Farage – even in a "semi-vegetative state" such as that which the ex-Ukip leader used to achieve after downing seven pints of Old Bastard in his pub.

Jeremy Corbyn WRITES

HELLO! It's me again. So here we go again! The hated western imperialist war machine is on the march again, all because Assad may – or may not – have used chemical weapons in his own back yard.

This is a complete overreaction, in my view. Geoff, the chap who rents the bit of allotment next to mine, has a tendency to use old bottles of bugspray, which don't have eco-friendly stickers on, on his marrows, but you don't catch me dropping missiles on his shed! Not yet, anyway!

Not that there's any proof that Assad's done anything wrong, oh no! May and Trump are always happy to blow things up first and ask questions later. They don't very slowly and ponderously go through proper procedures like me. Only last year I called for a UN investigation into who was responsible for the Syrian chemical attacks, which is the right thing to do. And when that UN investigation reported that Assad was definitely responsible, I immediately decided to call for a UN investigation into that UN investigation to discover who coerced them to come up with an answer that was clearly wrong.

This military action will accomplish nothing, and it's completely the wrong strategy. The correct strategy to accomplish nothing is to complain, obfuscate and call for endless resolutions that will never happen. That's my way to accomplish nothing and it's never let me down yet!

Here's what I propose. When all the unpleasantness has stopped, we should get round a big table with Assad's forces and the rebels and sort out their differences. Which is exactly the right time to do it, because by that time the only differences they'll have is one group will be alive and the other will be a bit dead, so I'm sure the talks will be quick and very productive!

Now, I'm feeling a little queasy so I'm going to go and lie down for a bit in my shed. I think I may have got pesticide poisoning, but I'm sure the UN will find out who's responsible eventually. My money's on Donald Trump!

Cheerio!

PS. I am eternally grateful to my good friend Diane Abbott for this totally accurate and completely authentic photo posted to Twitter of this week's raid by the US, as they mercilessly bombed the Syrian people.

PPS. Very disappointed by new film Murder on the Orient Express. Poirot decides that every passenger on the train was responsible for the crime. What nonsense! There was a Russian passenger on the train, played by Judi Dench, who was clearly innocent!

Pictures with New Titles, No.2

Fantoni (with apologies)

Girl in Nike Tracksuit, Matisse 1924

WETHERSPOON PUB CHAIN QUITS SOCIAL MEDIA

We don't want to be associated with places where people get tanked up and start fights

Let's Parlez Franglais!

Numéro 94

Le bombing de Syria

L'Entente War-dial!!

Emmanuel Macron: Bravo, moi-self! Courageusement, j'ai led les alliés to a grand triomphe dans le Middle-Est!

Thérèse Mai: Je was très courageuse aussi, vous know.

Macron: Et now, je suis très populaire en France. Oui, je suis la nouvelle Madame Thatcher. Syria est mon Falklands!

Mai: No, no, je suis la nouvelle Madame Thatcher qui will régne pour un autre dix ans!

Macron: Non, non, non, France est le country stuck in les 70s avec tout le monde on strike! Mais,

maintenant, le only type of strike qui matters est le missile strike! Vous gettez it? La guerre foreign will be mon sauveur!

Mai: Calmez-vous down, dear! C'est only a limited et proportionate missile attack!

Macron: Non, c'est une grande campagne militaire. Je suis le nouveau Napoléon!

Mai: Oui, just like in 1812 quand il a taken on les Russians et ça n'a pas fini trop bien pour lui!!

Macron: Ah! Perfide Albion!

Mai: Jumped up grenouille.

(La guerre des mots continue pendant 94 ans)

When Millennials Demonstrate

GOVERNMENT WELCOMES COMMONWEALTH LEADERS AMID WINDRUSH FURORE

I'm sure you'll understand that Mrs May has asked you all to be off the premises by 5pm

HOW THINGS CHANGE

1948	**2018**
WINDRUSH	**BUM'S RUSH**
Ship arrives bringing the first of a new generation of immigrants to help reconstruct Britain after the war	Ship departs taking all the immigrants unable to prove they've been living here sixty years

"The motivational speaker's just cancelled... he said he can't be arsed"

"It uses faecal recognition"

£50 FINE

PERCIVAL

Nursery Times

·············· Friday, Once-upon-a-time ··············

POISON ATTACK VICTIM WAKES UP

by Our Deadly Fruit Staff **Granny Smith**

THERE was delight in Nurseryland this week, as Snow White regained consciousness after falling victim to a brutal poison attack by an unknown assailant.

Nurseryland police are still looking for the mystery attacker, who was described as looking like an old Russian crone, with a heavy Russian accent, a big Russian hat and drinking Russian vodka, though there is no clue as to her country of origin.

The old not-necessarily-Russian witch was seen lurking outside Snow White's front door with a suspiciously shiny red apple, which turned out to have been laced with Novichok.

Snow White was only saved by the intervention of local dwarf medic, Doc.

Said Doc, "She was feeling Dopey and Sleepy, but now she's feeling Happy."

The crone/witch/queen/ tsarina expressed her joy that Snow White had recovered from the poisoned apple that she hadn't given her, but also expressed concern that poor little Snow White would not be safe around all the dangerous woodland creatures, bunnies, blue tits, fawns, butterflies and, of course, dwarves.

"Snow White would be far safer with me," she added, "living in the Magic Kremlin Castle, eating lovely apples every day, guarded by hungry Russian bears."

The Wicked Red Queen is believed to own a magic mirror and every day asks it: "Mirror, Mirror on the wall, who on earth shows a consistent pattern of behaviour of going round the world poisoning people they hate?"

And every day the Mirror says "You, Vladimir". (*Is this the fairest you can be? Ed.*)

PETER PAN SUES NBC OVER BREACH OF PRIVACY

by Our Media Staff **Wendy House**

PETER PAN, one of Nurseryland's biggest stars (second to the right, and straight on till morning) today flew into the High Court to demand damages from the Nurseryland Broadcasting Corporation for invading his privacy during a raid on his home by PC Plod.

PC Plod, who was looking for evidence of inappropriate behaviour with lost boys, has already apologised to Peter Pan and admitted that he'd fancied being on telly, so he'd alerted NBC who instantly despatched Budgie the Helicopter to film it all.

Peter Pan told the media, "This has cast a shadow over my life, which I had to ask Wendy to sew back on."

Asked to defend themselves, the NBC wept crocodile tears but insisted that it was in the public interest to show exciting helicopter raids on widescreen TV, adding in mitigation, "We never called him Paedo Pan, though we kind of implied it, if we're honest."

Peter Pan is 109, but looks 17.

WINDRUSH WOMAN OVERBOARD!

I've resigned? I had no idea

You were a useless Home Secretary

So, why aren't I Prime Minister?

Welcome to the Go-Home Office

There is now no hostile environment

Get lost!

Pack your bags!

We don't want your sort here!

'Humiliated and left jobless by Home Office officials'

by Our Windrush Correspondent **Dee Port**

A NEW victim of the Windrush Scandal has come forward, speaking of her brutal treatment at the hands of Home Office officials after a disagreement over paperwork led to her being left stateless.

"I trusted that the Home Office would look after me," said the woman who only wanted to give her name as Amber. "But they chose to leak papers to the Guardian showing that I didn't belong here and should be removed asap.

"It's humiliating being sent to the backbenches, a place I've barely set foot in since entering Westminster and I have no idea how to behave there. Yes, I probably should have seen the writing on the wall, but I never read anything that's written down."

The Home Office said it refused to comment on individual cases, such as Amber's, but did confirm that the targeted removal of politicians who think they can outmanoeuvre civil servant mandarins has always been central to the smooth running of the department.

"Have you been mis-sold a trip to the UK in the 1950s?"

'We're Back In The Black' Government's Shock Claim

by Our City Staff **Phil Spreadsheet**

A TREASURY spokesman last night astonished the world by announcing that the Government has now ended its controversial spending deficit.

"For the first time in decades," he said, "the Government is now in surplus, if you only count everyday running expenses and discount all the larger items.

"In fact, this year we are only having to borrow £42.6 billion, which is hardly anything.

"This means we are now on course to reduce the National Debt to a mere £1.86 trillion, which is only about four times what it was ten years ago.

"This shows that we are definitely in the black, so long as by 'black' you mean 'red'."

GOVERNMENT TO BAN STIRRERS

ECB proposes radical new tournament

by Our Cricket Correspondent
Noah Ball

THE English Cricket Board has announced a new tournament to turn around the fortunes of the sport and attract new fans to the game.

"This new version will differ from traditional cricket in that we'll be ditching all those tedious overs, bowlers, batsmen, stumps and wickets," said an ECB spokesman, "and replacing them with centre forwards, midfielders and goals. The new game will be called 'football'.

"But the essence of what makes cricket such an enthralling sport will remain, apart from the cricket bit, which as we all know is not suited to the millennial lifestyle.

"Our extensive ECB market research tells us the best way to win over non-cricket fans to the greatest game of all is to totally ditch all cricket from the competition entirely."

Apparently BY MIKE BARFIELD

MODERN SOCIAL PHENOMENA: A SUNDAY MORNING GUIDE

1. Interesting article here on 'mansplaining'...

2. Ah, yes, that's when a man patronisingly advises a woman on a subject with which she is already familiar – to her great annoyance...

3. Darling? Darling? ?

VISA CRISIS HITS WINDFALL GENERATION

by Our Home Office Staff **Chelsy Owner**

THERE was no outrage at all this week when the latest victims of hostility from the Home Office turned out to be Russian oligarchs from the so-called Windfall generation.

This term applies to a group of Putin's cronies who sailed over to Britain in their enormous yachts, with nothing but the clothes on their backs and a billion pounds in their pockets.

The Windfall generation have contributed hugely to their adopted country by creating endless jobs for solicitors, accountants and tax experts, not to mention London's world-famous laundry business.

They have also embraced our national culture by adopting football and ruining it. And what has their reward been? To be denied visas on the grounds that they are in some way dodgy.

These hard-working oligarchs have been denied entry and, in one case, a Mr Abramovich had to miss his own Cup Final with his own team winning.

However, the Home Office was unrepentant. "This is a genuinely

Immigrant on board the *Windrussian*

popular policy – we're cracking down and taking back control of one high profile visa. If he wants to see us, our door is always open, though we will check the handle before touching it."

CLARIFICATION: There is no evidence that Mr Abramovich has been involved in any illegal activity whatsoever. He is merely used as an example of the type of Russian person who might have been dodgy if he wasn't entirely innocent. Which he is.

● *This is a voluntary clarification and in no way cut and pasted from a threatening letter from top legal firm Will, Actfor & Anyone.*

"Too jolly?"

FEMALE STATUE STRIKES BLOW FOR EQUAL RIGHTS

You wash, I'll dry

COURAGE CALLS TO COURAGE EVERYWHERE

POETRY CORNER

In Memoriam
Sir Alex Ferguson,
legendary manager of
Manchester United

So. Farewell
Then Sir Alex Ferguson,
You have left the
Field of play.

Hang on, apparently
You haven't.
You have come back
From the dead,
Like Man United
So often did.

And now you
Are living in
Fergie Time.

E.J. Tribbute (17½ - nil)

"We met on wine"

S NEVIN

EXCLUSIVE TO ALL PAPERS

ARSENE WENGER – THE MAN WHO TRANSFORMED OUR NATIONAL GAME

by Our Football Staff **Phil Back-pages**

WHEN he arrived on these shores it was "Arsène Who?". But now he's known as Mr Arsenal, the revolutionary who turned football on its head.

Before Wenger's arrival, professional footballers would routinely sink 10 pints on the morning before the game, but Wenger, with one look through his professorial glasses, shrewdly realised that drinking a pint of water instead might make them less likely to throw up on the pitch at a crucial moment with the goal at their mercy.

It was also Strasbourg's soccer Svengali who lengthened the careers of his players by advising them to forego the pre-match kebab and try some stretching instead.

Even more radically, with his continental "five-a-day not 40-a-day" rule, he introduced the team to the notion of eating fruit and vegetables rather than

smoking two packs of Rothmans full-strength.

Wheezed one former pro, "At first I thought Broccoli was a left-back he'd signed from Inter Milan, but the boss soon put me right."

Of course the biggest change of all was when Wenger introduced foreign players to the Arsenal team to replace the British ones, which meant that Arsenal actually won something.

Now he is retiring, he leaves a gap in the game and we will all miss not being able to write articles saying, *"Why Wenger must go!"*

Arsène, with your urbane French ways, you have educated us all, so we say to you, Monsieur Wenger: Auf Weidersehen and Arrividerci.

ON OTHER PAGES

● How Wenger turned British football from an ugly, brutish, contact sport into the beautiful game that we know today, complete with diving, shirt-pulling and swearing at referees.

SALISBURY POISONING BREAKTHROUGH

■ NERVE agent was left on front door of Skripal's home. Police want to speak to Deliveroo driver seen in the area on Sunday, March 4

HOORAY FOR LOUIS!

MAY we be the first to congratulate the Cambridges on their choice of the name Louis for the latest addition to the Royal Family. Louis is an affectionate tribute to the late Lord Mountbatten and the name is steeped in royal history.

It is also associated with a number of French kings, all of whom were of course foreign and many of whom met a sticky end.

Was it really necessary to remind us of the excesses of the French ancien regime which led to poor Louis XVI having his head cut off?!

And then, of course, there is Louis, the king of the Swingers, in Disney's Jungle Book. Is this hairy simian from the subcontinent a suitable role model for the fifth in line to the British throne?

Or Louis Tomlinson, a member of the badly-behaved boy band One Direction? Is that what the Cambridges want, a dope-smoking deadbeat surrounded by unsuitable groupies?

Or the racing driver playboy Louis Hamilton *(You've got his name wrong. Ed.),* who goes around driving too fast, spraying champagne in people's faces and not paying his taxes whoops *(You're fired. Lord Rothermere, Prop.)*

Brit wins lottery jackpot

by Our Lotto Staff
Hugh Ro-millions

ONE of the biggest lottery prizes to be won in a random draw was today scooped by one lucky UK resident.

The winner of the chance-in-a-million, life-changing prize made his first public appearance with his mum and dad on the steps outside the Lindo wing of St Mary's hospital.

The recipient of the bumper bonanza prize was totally speechless, which is to be expected of a newly delivered baby.

"Despite his access to millions of pounds at such a young age, we are determined to keep him grounded," said his parents.

"He'll be treated no differently from any other prince of the realm, and we have every confidence that he will enjoy a normal royal upbringing, with all the complications that entails, before possibly celebrating his fourteenth birthday by being found drunk wearing a Nazi uniform in the gutter outside Chinawhite."

Said a spokesman for the royal family, "This confirms what we all knew: You have to be in it to win it!"

Exclusive to all newspapers

WHO ARE THE STRANGE NUTTERS WHO CAMP OUTSIDE THE LINDO WING WAITING FOR THE ROYAL BIRTH?

● It's us, of course.

© All newspapers.

SAUDIS LOCK UP WOMEN PROTESTORS

Stop moaning and drive yourself to prison

St Cakes to Slash Fees By Double

by Our Education Staff **Hugh Jafeez**

THE independent Midlands mixed-boarding school, St Cakes (motto: *Quis paget entrat*), has announced a bold new strategy to encourage a more diverse mix of pupils.

Said Headmaster, Mr Kipling, "We are taking a lead from that other great public school, St Owe, who have rightly noticed that middle-class parents can no longer afford to send their children to private schools which are now overrun by the offspring of Russian oligarchs and Chinese plutocrats."

Mr Kipling continued, "Here at St Cakes we consider this an excellent development and we have accordingly doubled our fees to encourage a wider range of extremely rich parent.

"New parents can rest assured that their children will not have to put up with any tiresome British children, particularly not those from middle-class homes."

He concluded, "There will, of course, still be bursaries for deprived and working-class children, in order for their photographs to feature in the prospectus in case the government is thinking of scrapping our charitable status."

St Cakes' current fees are £10,000 per day, which Mr Kipling described as "an exceedingly good sum".

Former pupils of St Cakes, Old Cakeians, include such luminaries as politician Simon Foggis, Junior Underminister for Paperclips in John Major's government, singer Tarquin Rubbish, who came seventh in the 2014 regional heats of *Britain's Got Talent*, and international banker Johnny Red-Trouser, who worked at global hedge fund manager Toxic & Loss before becoming a guest of Her Majesty in HMP Wandsworth.

TV TO WATCH

A Very English Scandal

Sunday 9pm (BBC1)

New BBC drama about charismatic Liberal toff Hugh Grant caught in an act of humbuggery.

Grant (played by the late Jeremy Thorpe) is discovered campaigning against press intrusion into privacy while acting in a TV series exposing the private lives of various public figures.

"In this day and age," said an unrepentent Grant, "we have a different attitude to humbuggery. Whereas in the past it might have been frowned upon, nowadays everyone is at it – especially me."

Don't miss cameo by Paddington Bear as Grant's lover, Norman Scott (*Is this right? Ed.*)

POETRY CORNER

In Memoriam the not-so-late Andrew Newton, hitman in the Jeremy Thorpe scandal (as seen on TV)

So. Not farewell
Then Andrew Newton.
You were famous for
Killing Rinka, the
Dog belonging to
Jeremy Thorpe's former
Lover, Norman Scott.

Everyone thought
You were very
Conveniently dead,
Including the police.

But now, miraculously,
You have been found,
Alive and well,
Living in Dorking.

Whatever next?
Will they find Rinka,
Alive and well,
Living quietly in a
Somerset dogs' home?

E.J. Thribb
(17½ or 122½ in dog years)

DIARY

GREETINGS, PRINCE LOUIS

SIR TIM RICE:

Welcome, young sir!
Who sets all our hearts a-stir!
More precious than myrrh!
And warmer than fur!
Goodly biddings, young Prince!
Tastier than after-dinner mints!
CHORUS: *So we won't say "Oh, Phooey!"*
No – we'll sing "Hurrah for Prince Louis!"

PIERS MORGAN: This morning I texted Louis to wish him the Best of British. He hasn't replied yet, but, frankly, I've noticed that all my best Royal buddies are a bit on the slow side when it comes to texting. I suppose they have to wait for a flunkey to do it for them! Louis is a smashing little guy and I look forward to introducing him to my good friends Michael Caine, Amanda Holden, Lord Sugar, Simon Cowell, Donald Trump and Rachel Stevens from S Club 7 over a pint or two in the years to come!

V.S. NAIPAUL: The new baby is a deep disappointment. Even after a week he has yet to do anything worthy of consideration. I struggle to think of a word to say in his favour. He has said nothing of interest. He cries and gurgles, gurgles and cries. These are clear signs of a peevish, unpleasant nature.

JACOB REES-MOGG: EXSULTATE! The universal jubilation surrounding the birth of His Royal Highness Prince Louis Arthur Charles makes it crystal clear that an overwhelming majority of the British people are in favour of pushing forward with Brexit. Furthermore, the joy exhibited by one's compatriots at this miraculous royal birth sends a message to the government that a complete break with the disastrous customs union is now not only desirable but obligatory.

AMANDA PLATELL: The old saying has it that Monday's child is "fair of face". Wrong! The first time I set eyes on Louis, coming out of the hospital with that know-it-all look as if he owned the place, I thought to myself, "Well, THIS Monday's child is fat of face". Time to shed a few pounds, chubby-chops! With all that money, you'd have thought Wills and Kate could have afforded a junior indoor rowing machine for him. I work out just a couple of hours a day and I'm told I have the body of a woman of 25. That's why men half my age are literally falling over themselves to take me on luxury five-star weekends in romantic hideaways. So face the facts, Prince. If you want me to be, in the iconic words of Billy Joel, your "Uptown Girl", then you'd best start cutting those cals – and fast!

Richard Dawkins @RichardDawkins
Just because the royal baby will be subjected by his grossly ill-informed parents to a grotesque "christening" does NOT mean that he will be more moral. Quite the opposite. Statistics show that people who define themselves as religious are more likely to be rapists, murderers and pickpockets. FACT.

JEFFREY ARCHER: With a few carefully-chosen words in the right ears, I managed to get The Duchess of Cambridge into the VIP Lindo Wing of St Mary's Hospital. Breathe not a word to anyone, but the Lindo Wing is actually named after me – Lord Jeffrey Lindo Archer. Little known fact, but it's my middle name. It's not something I boast about, but I dug deep in my pockets to have it built and equipped, and I secretly pay all the salaries of the splendid nurses and doctors, bless 'em. Before I became a Booker-winning author, I was actually a fully-qualified doctor, and I like to keep my hand in. I'm deeply proud to have been there to deliver Prince Louis last Monday. I wish I could have stayed longer, but I had promised to undertake a hush-hush assignment to rescue kidnapped twins in Mozambique in darkest South America – mission accomplished!

AFUA HIRSCH: Why bring race into the birth of a new "royal" baby? I'll tell you why. Because it's been there from the very beginning. As a young woman, Queen Elizabeth II could have married a leading black activist like Martin Luther King, who was her exact contemporary. But she chose not to. Instead, she married a rich white man – and, moreover, a rich white man whose not-so-distant ancestors lived and thrived in an empire founded on slavery and the forcible subjugation of the African people. Ditto, the Prince of Wales, who married two pampered rich white women in a row, rather than a brilliant humanitarian and political activist like Winnie Mandela. Prince Louis already has his hands full, eradicating the deep stain that attaches to his family's past. But we must never let him turn a blind eye to the problems of rising sea levels, drug trafficking, the continued persecution of the LGBTQ community, and a globalised economy that advantages rich white people – in fact, people just like him.

Sarah Ferguson @SarahTheDuchess
Thank you, gorgeous little Princepuppydog, for empowering us to believe that every day a dream is possible. And for spreading hope, love and literally lots of other great things around this beautiful world of ours…

OWEN JONES: Call me pernickety but it's a hard-won fact that the Establishment is hand-in-glove with the media to systematically employ royal births to distract our hard-won attention from the horrors facing the poor and dispossessed at home and abroad. They hope we will go all gooey over this latest royal birth of Prince Whoever so we won't want to know what's really happened to the Windrush victims. Transmitting falsehoods about a succession of royal babies to incite hatred against minorities is just the latest in a long line of closely-calibrated campaigns by the Tories and their allies to undermine the foundations of our hard-won democracy.

Sarah Ferguson @SarahTheDuchess
…Louis, you are my hero and I am so proud of your wisdom and inner strength. I just know you're going to love my new children's books Ballerina Rosie Goes Sailing and Budgie the Little Helicopter Goes Shopping now available from my bestest friends at amazon.co.uk.

As told to
CRAIG BROWN

Fallen angels

"They're not visitors, they're waiting for his bed!"

"She's free to go as soon as the doctor has seen her and the local authority has raised £8m to build and run a care home that can take her in"

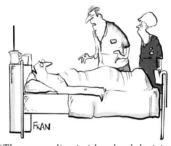

*"The new policy is 'devolved decision making'. What medication do **you** think you should have?"*

"When I grow up I want to be a nurse like Mummy and do filing"

"It's an EMERGENCY, get me forms 56D-3 and two 67Bs, together with a preliminary indication of budgetary implications"

"The operation was a great success, well within budget. Shame that your husband died"

MIDLIFE ISIS

I can't decide what to do next... behead a kaffir or buy a Volvo

★ SYRIAN TIMES ★

Friday 4 May 2018

THERE IS NO POINT – THE WAR IS LOST

by Our Labour Party Correspondent **Bashar Al-Assad**

WE ARE witnessing the final stages of a war which has been raging for years: but ultimately, it is over.

Any intervention by foreign governments at this point is pointless. The Labour Party is completely in the grip of Jeremy Corbyn, and the firing of a few rockets by disgruntled Blairites will only serve to cause a few minor casualties here and there.

Even if we wanted to intervene, and provide armaments to the rebels, which

faction should we support? David Miliband? Tony Blair? Let's be honest. The idea of a moderate, centrist opposition to Mr Corbyn is a fantasy. The only people left are the sort of zealots and maniacs, like Owen Smith, whom it would be desperately irresponsible to arm.

There will be no way of causing final peace in the region without finding out what Mr Corbyn wants, and then giving it to him. Any attempt at resistance is completely futile and that is all there is to be said on the matter.

"No, I'm not being stalked, officer – my husband keeps following me since he recently retired"

Israel to host Eurovision and WW3

by Our Eurovision Correspondent **Neil Points**

A spokesman for the Israeli Government has said they are extremely excited that their country been chosen as the location in 2019 for both Eurovision and World War Three: "Both are events which have a huge worldwide brand, and both will have millions glued to their screens, some in total horror at the mounting atrocities and bombs, and others marvelling at the fireworks.

"We are preparing for a huge amount of terrible acts. And people singing badly too.

"We are confident that Eurovision will put Israel on the map. And that World War Three will take Palestine off the map."

Venue confirmed

"We've already chosen the venue for Eurovision 2019 – it's the American embassy in Jerusalem," continued the Israeli spokesman.

"The audience will watch from inside, in a specially built blast-proof area, while artistes will perform outside in a large, flattened area of real estate which we've discovered will be made commercially available by Mr Trump for 2019. Apparently, it's called the Gaza strip."

The news unleashed wild scenes of celebration on the occupied West Bank, bringing both heavily armed Israeli security forces and stick-waving Palestinians onto the streets.

"Surely this is what Eurovision is all about," said one Israeli sniper. "Lots of different cultures, some armed like us, some unarmed like them. It's great to bring people together, because when they get closer it's easier to shoot 50 of them dead."

THE LESSONS OF HISTORY

"We must win the war against knife crime"
says Home Secretary 2018

"We must tackle the scandal of knife crime"
says Home Secretary 2015

"It is time to halt the tragic spread of knife crime"
says Home Secretary 2013

Home Secretary issues ultimatum on rising tide of knife crime 2010

Home Secretary's 25-point plan for solving knife crime crisis in full 2005

"Massive crack-down on unprecedented knife-related crime wave" promises Home Secretary 1981

Alarming outbreak of knife-related homicide in East End. Home Secretary promises capture of the so-called "Ripper" 1889

Pippa's Pregnancy Tips

YES, it's Pippa Middleton's handy guide on how to get pregnant.

1 Say "Hiya" to some fit guy in maroon trousers

2 Say "Wow, you're Spennie's brother from Made In Chelsea"

3 Order second bottle of Fizzington

4 Order Uber

5 Can't quite remember rest

6 Hey presto, you're preggers!

NEXT WEEK: How to raise a family in six easy steps

UP, UP, UP…
70 80 90!
BRITAIN'S BANK HOLIDAY BREAKS ALL RECORDS

by Our Bank Holiday Staff
May Day

AS the thermometer last week soared to unprecedented levels, London's young people celebrated the heat- wave in their own unique way.

With every hour that passed, another knife crime pushed the 2018 total to a new high. 70, 80, 90… and still the figures carried on *(cont. p94)*

(cont. p94)

HOW DOES JUMPIN' JEZZA STILL DO IT, AT HIS AGE?
by **Mick Jagger**

AT 75, most people would be happy pottering about on their allotment and playing the occasional game of bowls – but not the amazing Jezza, whose idea of retirement is to go out on the road with his band and trot out those Seventies hits to an audience of literally tens of screaming fans.

And even if you're a bit bored of the old hits (Northern Ireland, Venezuela, Israel), there's no denying that he is in remarkable shape for a man his age.

When you see him moving slowly around the stage like a man of only 71, it is difficult to believe that he was strutting his stuff way back before the Rolling Stones had even been invented.

Yet still the groupies love him and the women go weak at the knees when Jezza mentions renationalising the water board. No wonder that the world's greatest frontman is *(cont. age 94)*

(cont. age 94)

Jeremy Corbyn WRITES

HELLO! It's me again. Well I don't know what you lot are waiting for! Didn't you know that tickets for Labour Live, AKA Jezfest are on sale RIGHT NOW?

I have to say, the phones are ringing off the hook with people making enquiries. They keep asking how many tickets we've sold and then ringing off extremely quickly when we tell them. So the interest is through the roof, daddio!

(I must point out in the interests of sexual equality that there are also mummios, who are just as cool as daddios and do much good work in the community raising kiddios).

At 'Jezfest' our watchword is variety. Whether you like Owen Jones reading his angry 'Tony Bliar' poems, John McDonnell doing his amusing Morrissey covers ('Hang the MP' is my fave!) or just Billy Bragg wandering onstage and looking tired, there's something for everyone!

But fun and games aside, 'Jezfest', of course will mainly cater to fans of Jez. I will be performing all forms of Jez. I'll be doing Trad Jez (me reminiscing happily about Castro), Cool Jez (where I'm asked my opinion on Syrian war crimes) Hot Jez (where I'm asked my position on Israeli war crimes), Free-form Jez (where I improvise a question for PMQs for a few hours) or just Jez and Blues (where I explain how I whip my MPs to abstain on Brexit and let the Tories do what they like).

What you will notice almost immediately is there will be a lot of empty chairs around you. That does not mean that these are unsold tickets, oh dear no! What has happened is we have flown in many thousands of chairs as a gesture of solidarity with the folding garden chairmakers of Russia.

So here's to a sold-out concert and a defiant blow against capitalism!

It's a win-win! Especially when UNITE are bailing us out! Thanks lads, don't forget when we sing Oh-Je-re-my Cor-byn at the end, raise your lighters and set fire to those Union fees!

Cheerio!

PS. You may have noticed that I have been calling for a united Ireland! What ever next, a united Labour Party?

Puritan Streak

DUMB BRITAIN

Real contestants, real quiz shows, real answers, real dumb!

Tipping Point, ITV

Ben Shephard: Which London landmark houses Big Ben?
Contestant: Tower Bridge.

Shephard: The Dolomites are a branch of which major European mountain range?
Contestant: The Grand Canyon.

Shephard: Released in 1967, which tusked animal completes the title of the Beatles song "I Am the…" what?
Contestant: Elephant.

Shephard: Which Biblical figure do Christians believe is the son of God sent to save mankind from death and sin?
Contestant: Pass.

Shephard: Native to Africa, the mandrill is the largest and most colourful of which primate?
Contestant: I'm literally going to say lion.

Shephard: In 1649, which English war resulted in the beheading of Charles I?
Contestant: World War One.

Shephard: Which famous military organisation was set up by King Alfred the Great in the ninth century?
Contestant: The SAS.

Shephard: The fabled city of El Dorado was said to be made of which metal?
Contestant: Tin.

Shephard: The Sienese school of painting flourished in which city?
Contestant: Rome.

Shephard: Born in Trier in Germany in 1818, what was the first name of the political philosopher Marx?
Contestant: Umm, Howard?

Shephard: The word "loop" is an anagram of which horse-based sport?
Contestant: Pool.

Shephard: On what date is Christmas Day celebrated each year?
Contestant: Wednesday.

Pointless, BBC1

Alexander Armstrong: Can you give me the name of a medallist from the Rio Olympics?
Contestant: Mo... Mowlam.

Armstrong: Name a member of the Conservative cabinet in 2016.
Contestant: Nigel Farage.

Armstrong: We're looking for the name of any country in the world that doesn't have the letters W, O, R, L and D in it.
Contestant 1: The Ganges.
Contestant 2: Alaska.

Cash Trapped, ITV

Bradley Walsh: Which leader of the Labour party died in 1994 and was succeeded by Tony Blair?
Contestant: Maggie Thatcher.

Walsh: Who won four gold medals at the 1936 Olympics in Berlin?
Contestant: Usain Bolt.

The Chase, ITV

Bradley Walsh: What is the most commonly used food energy unit around the world?
Contestant: Potato.

Walsh: Who wrote their 1653 book *The Compleat Angler*?
Contestant: J.R. Hartley.

Walsh: "Down With Big Brother" is a quote from which George Orwell novel?
Contestant: 1986.

Walsh: From which animal does venison come?
Contestant: A young horse.

Walsh: In which film did Charlton Heston play Moses?
Contestant: Lawrence of Arabia.

Walsh: In 1841, Thomas Cook's first package tour from Leicester to Loughborough used which form of transport?
Contestant: The tube.

Walsh: What day of the week rhymes exactly with Sunday?
Contestant: Tuesday.

Walsh: Which saint is revered by Christians as the forerunner of Jesus Christ?
Contestant: St Nicholas.

Walsh: Who awarded the Presidential Medal of Freedom to Joe Biden in January 2017?
Contestant: George Washington.

Walsh: What is another name for the Victoria and Albert Museum?
Contestant: The Science Museum.

Walsh: Which former Soviet leader appeared in a commercial for Pizza Hut?
Contestant: Boris Johnson.

Walsh: Which "mad monk" was born in Siberia in about 1869?
Contestant: Confucius.

Walsh: What kind of animal was Roy Rogers' companion Trigger?
Contestant: Bear.

Walsh: Which British king was Prince Michael of Kent's grandfather?
Contestant: Henry VIII.

Walsh: Brueghel the Elder painted the biblical character Jonah leaving which sea creature?
Contestant: The Loch Ness Monster.

Walsh: Robbie Burns's poem starts, "My love is like a red red…"
Contestant: Wine.

Walsh: What primary colour is the aperitif Martini Rosso?
Contestant: Green.

Walsh: The Russian republic of Chechnya is in which mountain range?
Contestant: The Alps.

Walsh: Which major river joins the Brahmaputra in Bangladesh?
Contestant: The Danube.

Walsh: What is the only stroke in a swimming medley that doesn't begin with the letter B?
Contestant: Backstroke.

Walsh: What dairy product was one of the first foods rationed during 1940?
Contestant: Spam.

Walsh: Which British prime minister attended an all-female college at Oxford?
Contestant: Tony Blair.

Walsh: Which historical figure signed his name "Guido"?
Contestant: William Shakespeare.

Celebrity Mastermind, BBC1

John Humphrys: What sea separates the east coast of Britain from Norway?
Celebrity: The Pacific.

Humphrys: The female flowers of climbing plant *humulus lupulus* are very important in giving beer its bitter flavour. What are they?
Celebrity: Hydrangeas.

Humphrys: What does the MI stand for in MI5 and MI6?
Celebrity: Mission Impossible.

Humphrys: What pantomime, usually set in China, is taken from a story in the Arabian Nights?
Celebrity: *Withnail and I.*

Tenable, ITV

Warwick Davis: Name any of the last ten monarchs of the United Kingdom.
Contestant 1: Elizabeth III.
Contestant 2: Elizabeth I.
Contestant 3: Charles II.
Contestant 4: William V.

The Boss, BBC1

Susan Calman: What name is given to an Egyptian camel with one hump?
Contestant: A unihump.

Alphabetical, ITV

Jeff Stelling: Initials of a Rolling Stones hit from 1966... P.I.B.
Contestant: Puss In Boots.

Metro Radio, Newcastle-upon Tyne

Host: Crotchets, minims and quavers are examples of what?
Caller: Crisps.

BBC WM

Danny Kelly: What is the full name of the English county known as Northants?
Caller: Kent.

Perfection, BBC2

Nick Knowles: Lord Lucan was buried in Westminster Abbey. True or false?
Contestant: True.

Hardball, BBC1

Ore Oduba: Merino wool comes from which animal?
Contestant: The whale.

Oduba: What animal is a cross between a horse and a donkey?
Contestant: A honkey.

The £100K Drop, All 4

Davina McCall: Which of these three events of World War II happened most recently: the Dunkirk evacuation, the Battle of Britain, or the D-Day Normandy landings?
1st contestant: I've never heard of the Battle of Britain.
2nd contestant: I think the Normandy landings were in the 1920s.
Together: Let's go £5,000 Dunkirk evacuation and £2,500 Battle of Britain.

Exclusive to all papers

The 10 key moments of Royal wedding

By Phil Space

1 The moment the editor texted me and said, "Why didn't you know who designed the dress, you idiot?"

2 The moment the editor said, "I want a thousand words on how cheeky Charlotte upstaged grumpy George in the Battle of the Bridesmaids"

3 The moment the editor asked me, "Can you lip-read? I don't care, just make it up"

4 The moment I googled, "Who designed Victoria Beckham's dress?"

5 The moment the chief sub said they'd spiked my 2,000-word piece on fascinators on the grounds that it wasn't at all fascinating

6 The moment I confessed I'd never seen 'Suits' and had no idea who anyone was

7 The moment I wrote a piece criticising Mr Mumford for not turning up with any of his sons

8 The moment the editor said, "You've confused Meghan's mum with Oprah Winfrey"

9 The moment I was fired by the editor

10 The moment I was rehired by all the other papers, to write even more of this bilge.

The Beckhams

David   Victoria

Speech bubbles: "When's the next big Royal event?" — "That's a bit tactless in front of Pater" — "How long is the honeymoon...?" — "...until the tabloids turn on you" — "Smile! Watch the Fergie!"

By Royal Appointment… GNOME MINI-MART

A round-up of all the merchandise now available at half-price after its incredibly successful launch last week

Royal Wedding Chess Set

FEATURING a black bishop who moves about in all directions.

£9.99

Bishop Curry Powder

HOT AND FIERY

JUST LIKE THE SERMON! FEEL THE HEAT IN YOUR HEART!

£1.99 per kilo

Panini Harry's Exes Sticker Album

COLLECT them and swap them with your mates, just like Harry did! **Includes album and first set of stickers** (Cressida, Chelsy, etc). **£1.99** *plus introductory sticker pack of 50.*

PANINI — Harry's Exes

Elton John Wig'n'Glasses

NOW you and your partner can gatecrash any event. And play the piano! Weddings, funerals, you name it, just slip on the **Elton John Wig'n'Glasses** comedy combo   **99p**

GINGER NUTS

ROAR with laughter as you remember the best man's speech which no one heard, but which might have included a near-the-knuckle ginger reference.
£4,589.00

Kay Burley Horror Mask

WANT TO RUIN AN EVENT? Simply get over-excited, don your **Kay Burley mask** and hey presto! YOU'VE ANNOYED EVERYONE!
Free with Sky subscription

THE AMAL CLOONEY SKY DISH

WHATEVER the occasion, you can watch Sky Sports in style with this incredible development in millinery-based satellite TV technology. **£200 per month**
(not including installation or George Clooney)

The James Corden cordon

VIP security cordon that keeps out unwanted guests, apart from James Corden. **£20.18**

DIANA SEAT

YOUR OWN empty seat, dedicated to the late Princess of Hearts. Leave it out at any event and it's just like she's with you.
£374.84

Daily Mail

Monday, May 21, 2018

WHY OH WHY DID THEY LET THAT WACKY BLACK BISHOP TRY TO STEAL THE SHOW?

asks Quentin Lettshavesomethingreallyboringinstead

I REALLY can't understand why everyone seems to be going on about Bishop Curry, the arm-waving Chicago preacher who was apparently the star of the royal wedding.

I am sure I am not alone in thinking that this exhibitionistic holy roller was just about the most embarrassing thing I had ever seen in a pulpit.

For a staggering 14 minutes he ranted on, to the obviously growing distress of Her Majesty the Queen who was forced to sit stony-faced in front of a histrionic display such as she could never have imagined witnessing in all her 66 years as head of the Church of England.

Surely we must now all agree that to invite this joke figure to participate in such a solemn ceremony was a catastrophic misjudgement.

What the occasion called for, in my view, was a sober and serious sermon properly suited to this historic moment in our nation's story.

How much better it would have been if the Archbishop of Canterbury had fulfilled his traditional duty by preaching instead the kind of sermon that the Church of England has excelled in providing for such occasions for many centuries.

All I could think of as I squirmed in my armchair at the self-regarding hammy theatrics of the right-on bishop was how much more appropriate it would have been to hear the Most Reverend and Right Honourable the Lord Archbishop of Canterbury, Justin Welby, standing before us in properly dignified fashion saying, "You know, in a very real sense, the coming together of these two young persons must remind us on the one hand of the wedding at Cana, described in the Gospel according to St John, and on the other of the wonderful lyrics of that celebrated 'grime artist' Mr Stormzy, one of whose works I was listening to this morning on my way here in preparation for the happy event.

"And you know, there is a line in that song that says, 'I stay prayed up and get the job done'."

(At this point, our columnist Mr Letts unfortunately suffered a heart attack and had to be removed to intensive care by a team of volunteers from the St John Gospel Ambulance choir, singing that perennial wedding favourite "Stand By Your Man".)

The Guardian

Monday, 21 May, 2018

Why oh why didn't Harry and Meghan wear seatbelts?

by Our Royal Correspondent
Joy Kill

There's only one real question that people should be asking as the nation basks in this sickeningly deluded infantile national fantasy.

What on earth were Harry and Meghan thinking of, as they blithely drove off in their overpriced, oh so "eco-friendly" electricity-guzzler? What sort of role models are they? What sort of example are they setting to ordinary, diverse, inclusive working or non-working men and women or those who define themselves simply as non-gender specific car passengers?

Apparently, if you're entitled and privileged, you don't have to obey the laws of the land, on the grounds that you don't have to obey the law on private land, such as Windsor. Given that the Royal family own the entire country, why stop there? And why did none of the thousands of police officers deployed at public expense breathalyse Harry and Meghan, who had clearly been drinking at the reception?

Meghan, moreover, must be the first black person in a car not to be stopped by the police, on the very day she became Duchess of Sussex. Coincidence? I think not.

Far be it from the Guardian to pour water on this joyous event, but the photos we really want to see are those of Harry and Meghan in police custody, answering charges of dangerous driving.

I don't want to bring this up again, because surely Harry has suffered enough, but has he learned nothing from the tragic death of his mother, who was not wearing a seatbelt? This is the only important issue of the entire farrago and it's no good pretending that you're interested in the dress, or the guest list or details of DJ Idris Elba's playlist.

THOSE TELLING ROYAL ASIDES THAT OUR LIP READER PICKED UP

Bet that bastard Dacre hires a lip reader

What will happen now that Meghan has changed Britain forever

DAY 1 Meghan ends racism

DAY 2 Meghan solves gender inequality

DAY 3 Meghan cures cancer

DAY 4 Meghan walks on water

DAY 5 Meghan coaches England to World Cup victory

DAY 6 Meghan sorts Brexit

DAY 7 Papers admit they may have over-hyped how Meghan has changed Britain forever

The Eye's guide to those Royal-themed wedding cocktails, served up at the Frogmore House party to end all parties

by The Man Who Was Definitely There

HERE ARE THE TOP TEN

Vodka Markletini

Sloe Gin gerbloke

Princess Margarita

Banana Equerry

Bloody Fergie

Tom Parker Bowles Collins

Elton Johnnie Walker

Pippa Colada

Becks Fizz

Victoria Sour

George Clooney's Nespresso Martini™

Rum and Coke without the rum
(are you sure about this? Ed. – doesn't matter, I've made the rest up as well)

Kir Starmer Royale
(he wasn't there. Ed – I told you I've made this up)

Sarah Vain

Putting the Me in Meghan!!

OK, we all enjoyed that wedding. The sun shining, happy crowds, young couple in love – what's not to like?

Well, those preening celebs for a start, busily taking selfies of themselves all over the place. How self-obsessed can you get?

B-list actresses from American TV series that no one's ever seen. Footballers, designers, pop singers. What sort of a crowd is that to invite to a historic national occasion?

I know some people have said it was a refreshing change not to have any politicians on the wedding list this time.

But surely it was a mistake not to have at least one heavyweight cabinet minister to represent Her Majesty's government, preferably one with a photogenic wife who is an expert on fashion and could have been relied on to come up with something elegant but appropriate for the day.

And I can tell you, had such a person been invited, she wouldn't have been rushing round taking selfies of herself with other famous people.

No, she would have a thoughtful and brilliant piece ready, saying all that needed to be said about the day in the *Daily Mail* – headlined "I Was There and the Rest of You Weren't", by award-winning columnist Sarah Vain.

***

THE Speaker John Bercow has got into trouble for describing that dreadful old cow Andrea Leadsom as a "stupid woman".

What's wrong with that? For once, Bercow has got it spot on.

Mrs Leadballoon is so stupid that she even stood against Mrs May for the leadership of the Tory party, when quite obviously the only candidate who could have beaten Theresa and become the greatest prime minister the country has ever known was my hubby, Mr Gove!

***

I'LL tell you something else about that wedding. Did you see Fergie's daughters looking badly-dressed and out of place amongst all those glamorous, beautifully-dressed A-list celebs?

If only they'd invited me instead of the two dumpy, lumpy and frumpy princesses, the whole day would have gone much better.

POETRY CORNER

**In Memoriam
Eric Bristow, darts legend**

So. Farewell
Then Eric Bristow.
They called you
"The Crafty Cockney".

You are going
Up the Apples
And Pears to the
Pearly Gates,
As sadly, at 60,
You are
Brown Bread.

Yes, "Treble Twenty"
Was your score,
In more ways
Than one.

You were very
Straight talking,
To the point
Of offensive,
No bull.

You loved to drink,
You loved to smoke,
You loved a curry,
Who'd have thought
You'd be taken
From us
So late.

       E.J. Thribb
    (17½ pints a night)

**In Memoriam
Ken Dodd,
entertainer**

So. Farewell
Then Ken Dodd.

They say you used
To go on forever,
But, sadly, that
Wasn't true.

They also said
Only two things in
Life are certain –
Death and Taxes.

Unfortunately,
You only
Avoided
One.

And now it's
Knotty Ashes
To ashes.

       E.J. Thribb
  (£17½m in suitcases)

**In Memoriam
Tom Wolfe, the greatest
writer of the 20th century,
apart from Philip Roth**

So. Farewell
Then Tom Wolfe,
Founder of
"the New Journalism"
And author of
Radical Chic and
*The Kandy-Kolored
Tangerine-Flake
Streamline Baby*.

You were, however,
Best known for
Your book (and later film)
About astronauts,
The Right Stuff,
And for always
Wearing a
White suit.

Now that you
Yourself have gone
Into the heavens,
Will you be
Wearing white
For eternity?

       E.J. Thribb (17½)
  Author of *The White Stuff*

**In Memoriam
Rodney Bewes,
David Cassidy,
AC/DC's Malcolm Young
and Charles Manson**

So. Farewell
Then quite a lot
Of people.

*Whatever Happened
To The Likely Lads?*
Well, in your case, Rodney,
Now we know.

*Could It Be
Forever?*
Sorry David,
No.

Malcolm, let's hope
You're not on the
Highway to Hell.

But we know who
Definitely is,
Don't we, Charles?

       E.J. Thribb (17½)

PLOT AGAINST MAY

So we put this on her doorknob!

'This was our best night ever' says everyone

by Our Political Staff
Nonna Vent

IN ONE of the most remarkable democratic earthquakes ever to rock the world of local politics, nothing much happened.

All parties were quick to claim a historic victory despite the evidence to the contrary.

A Labour spokesperson was first onto the TV screens, claiming "Labour has not had such a stunning performance since we took control of Neasden in 1953. That spelt the end of the Tories for good and the revival of Labour under charismatic council leader Sidney (later Sir Sidney) Noggis."

The Tories, however, poured cold water on Labour's claims and immediately countered with a string of interviews on Breakfast TV.

"The fact that we didn't lose Richtown in Surrey and Poshworth in South London is proof that we Tories did better than any other mid-term government since we didn't lose Neasden in 1932, which led directly to a Tory council administration under the charismatic leader Piers (later Lord) Foppington-Toppington."

Only the Liberal Democrats kept a sense of proportion, with their spokesman telling his partner, "Realistically, when you look at all the results and the outrageous claims of the mainstream parties, this was a night of spectacular success for the Lib Dems. Not since we came a remarkable third in Neasden in 1907, under the charismatic Sandy Beard (later Prisoner 747324) have we performed this well and the night of Thursday 3 May signals the ultimate Lib Dem comeback."

"Some day, son, all this will be yours"

■ ANT??!! Dontchahatehim!!??!! He's the drink-driving love rat who's dumped his missus for her best friend!!?! Talk about having Ant in your pants!!? Geddit??! When it came to his marriage it was "I'm a celebrity, get me out of here!!?" And when it comes to being a top class, grade 'A' bastard, yes, "Britain's Got Talent". Ant and Dec??!! Ant and <u>Deceit</u>, more like!!?

■ ANT??! Dontchaluvhim!!??!! Why shouldn't he find a little love and happiness after all he's been through??!! And if that takes the shape of the friend of Mrs Ant in his pants then so be it!!?? Auntie Glenda gives them her blessing!!?! Leave him alone, I say, and let this celebrity get out of his dark place and show Britain he's got real talent again!!?? Ant and Dec??!! More like Ant and <u>Decency</u>!!?? *(This is terrible, keep going, Ed.)*

■ OK, so the bloke from Game of Thrones got married to the girl who was in it as well!!??!! Who cares??!! Do you think we're interested, Mr Harrington?!! "You know nothing John Snow!!!" And when they threw all that confetti on the bride's head it looked like winter was coming!!?? Geddit??!! Game of Thrones???! Game of Drones more like??!! Z-z-z-z-z-z.

■ Kit 'n' Rose!??! What a great white wedding and not a red one, like in the series where everyone got murdered. Don't know what I'm talking about, readers??!! Then "you know nothing" and you should be aware that "winter is coming". Can't wait for the next series of Game of Thrills. *(You're fired, Ed.)*

■ HEY Mr Pressman!??! Time to stop a-moanin' and a-groanin' about female football pundits!! Why shouldn't the gals drone on like the fellas??!! "He shoots. He scores. Or maybe he misses." You see??! Anyone can do it!!?! It's time for equal opportunity to be boring!!?? Gizza job Mr Telly, I'll be Gaby Lineker??! Geddit??!!

■ Lenny Henry??!! Now it's Leany Henry. OK, so he's lost weight??!! I've lost interest and the will to live…

■ *HERE THEY ARE – Glenda's World Cup Willies?!?! (in a non-sexist way)*

● Poldark!?!! OK, so Aidan Turner isn't playing in the World Cup, but I'd like to see him taking off an England shirt!?? Phwoar!!?!

● Poldark!?!! OK, he's still not a footballer, but he's doing a new play. Let's hope the investors don't lose their shirts but Aidan *does* in the first act!?? Phwoar!!?!

● Poldark!?!! OK, I concede, he has nothing whatsoever to do with the World Cup, but he can come round and score in my box any time he *(That's quite enough, Ed.)*

Byeee!!

More apply for Love Island than Oxbridge

THERE was widespread shock yesterday over the news that considerably more young people had applied for something that probably wouldn't happen but would be a bit of a laugh and something to tell their mates about, than something which requires top-level academic qualifications and is guaranteed to leave them with debts of up to £50,000.

One Cambridge don told the Eye, "Of course we'd all like to go on telly and show off all summer and then come out with a Damehood at the end of it, but quite frankly, only Mary Beard can get a look-in with the casting people."

POLDARK AUDITION LATEST

We'll let you know… Next!

HISTORIC KOREAN PEACE BANQUET

They've eaten the dogs of war

KOREAN SUMMIT RAISES HOPES OF PEACE TALKS

by Our Diplomatic Staff **Hans Shake**

THE historic summit meeting of North Korea's Kim Jong-un and South Korea's Moon Jae-in, which saw the two leaders set aside decades of bitter hatred, has raised fresh hopes in the village of Great Budworth in Cheshire that Leave voter Gordon Matthews and his Remain-voting son Freddie might one day speak again.

"Gordon and Freddie haven't spoken one word to each other since Christmas 2016 when an argument about the merits of EU freedom of movement turned nasty and Gordon ended up with the gravy bowl in his lap before

he stormed out," said Freddie's mum, Beryl.

"Last Christmas, things got even more strained when Freddie announced he'd be spending the holidays with his girlfriend's parents in New Malden, as at least her dad wasn't a Farage-loving crypto-fascist.

"Inspired by the Korean summit, I have arranged for a historic meeting between Gordon and Freddie to take place next month in the demilitarised zone of Nan's house, where I hope to broker a peace agreement and bring hostilities to an end over some spag bol and a few cans of cider."

GRENFELL INQUIRY

Why Was There So Much Money To Burn?

As the hugely-paid lawyers and experts began their two-year investigation with two weeks of non-legal remembrance, there were repeated warnings that a vast amount of taxpayers' money would go up in flames with no result.

"It's a financial disaster just waiting to happen," said one expert. "The warning signs are all there and they've got entirely the wrong type of panel *(That's enough bad taste. Ed.)*

IN CASE OF WEAPON ATTACK...

Nursery Times

END OF THE LINE FOR FAT CONTROLLER

by Our Transport Staff **Rev Tawdry**

THE Nurseryland Toy Railway Network was rocked today by the shocking news that the Fat Controller is to give up running the controversial Wicked Witch of the East Coast Line.

After only a couple of years, the line has done so badly that the formerly Fat Controller has lost so many pounds, he is now the Thin Controller.

"I thought fleecing members of the public who have no choice would be a piece of cake," he said, "but it turned out that even running it badly is really hard work and costs a stack."

The Thin Controller said the stress of cancelling trains and rewriting timetables had added to making him even more of a skeleton, just like the service, and he was delighted to hand it back to the Nurseryland government, even though they didn't want it.

Said employee Thomas the Tank Engine, "This decision has been a very long time coming, people have been waiting for it for ages and ages, and we were worried that it would just be cancelled."

Ronald the Replacement Bus Service added, "This isn't the first time this has happened – let's just hope this opportunity to improve the service doesn't go off the rails/hit the buffers/ end up in a siding!"

Meanwhile train services were no better in the South of Nurseryland, with a new

timetable adding to the chaos, although many commuters said it was hard to tell. The revised timetable is as follows:

- 08.00 New timetable comes into effect
- 08.01 First train cancelled
- 08.15 Second train cancelled
- 09.23 Third train arrives too crowded for anyone to get on
- 09.25 Fourth train cancelled due to commuter on line
- 09.45 Work starts on new timetable
- 10.15 Rail network posts inappropriately cheerful tweet: "Sorry folks, it's Meltdown Monday."
- 10.17 Rail network tweets warning to commuters of "Tits-Up Tuesday, Woeful Wednesday, Thank-God-It's-Not-Friday Thursday, and Fucking Friday."

RAIL TIMETABLE CHAOS

I was the Girl On The Train when I started out

HISTORIC SUMMIT: A TRIUMPH FOR DIPLOONACY

"It's so nice to meet somebody normal"

Nursery Times

Friday, Once-upon-a-time

HIT REALITY SHOW RETURNS TO NURSERYLAND

by Our TV Sex Staff **Robin Cock**

THE popular TV show *Love Ratings Island* is back on our screens, and this time the line-up of unlikely couples will blow your mind.

After last year's rollercoaster series in which Owl and Pussycat netted a £5 prize after their scandalous scenes in the pool in an inflatable pea-green boat, this year's offering promises to be the most sizzling and sex-drenched yet.

Early frontrunners are the Dish and the Spoon, who are already at it like knives, talking about running away together while spooning and looking dishy.

Georgie Porgie is looking increasingly unlikely to couple up with anyone, having already kissed all the girls on the island (where the Bonk Tree grows) on day one and making them cry. Jack and Jill were last seen going up the hill together for a bit of furtive water-gathering and they're expected to have a tumble later.

Also in the running are the Princess and the Frog, although they have yet to kiss, which may change everything.

The spider's chances of hooking up with Little Miss Muffet look slight, after he startled her at breakfast by sitting down beside her unannounced when she was eating her curds and whey.

The Emperor has impressed no one by strutting around in his new clothes, pointing out how fit and ripped he is, though he is wearing more than all the other contestants.

Goldilocks has been labelled a slut by some of the other contestants for sleeping in the beds of three different bears.

When asked whether the winning couple would actually fall in love and live happily ever after, the producers of the show said, "Don't be silly, what do you think this is, a fairytale?!"

"Go away, I'm busy."

Batman and Rodin

Corbyn calls for return of marbles

by Our Political Staff
Andrew Marrbles

THE leader of the Labour Party, Mr Jeremy Corbyn, on a visit to Athens last week, demanded the immediate repatriation of the so-called "marbles" that have caused such bad feeling over the years.

Said Jeremy Corbyn, "I lost my marbles in the 1960s and it's time I got them back. My marbles belong in my head and nowhere else. The loss of my marbles has been a national disaster and left the once proud Labour Parthenon in ruins."

Critics, led by the late Lord Elgin, claimed that, on the contrary, the Corbyn marbles were better off in a museum as a reminder of a bygone era.

Lord Elgin said, "The Corbyn marbles should be kept safe under lock and key where they can no longer do any damage to anyone."

But the British Labour leader was adamant, stating, "Only by the restoration of my marbles will I be able to become a truly national treasure and unite Britain once again."

"You are charged with taking sexual advantage of numerous women by cynically exploiting your status as a handsome young man with a magnetic personality"

CHRIS MADDEN

Brexiteers Welcome Doomsday Scenario

by Our Brexit Staff **Cliff Edge**

Leading pro-Brexit MPs have hailed the leaked civil service report outlining the worst-case, no-deal scenario as "good news for Britain".

Said David Davis, the Brexit Secretary from whose department the controversial document was passed to journalists, "Project Fear has failed yet again because these so-called warnings are in fact an enormous boost for post-Brexit Britain."

He continued, "The report says there will be immediate shortages of food, fuel and medicine. That is a hugely positive outcome for obvious reasons:

1. Lack of food means an end to the obesity crisis.

2. Fuel shortages mean less pollution and a radical improvement in air quality.

3. With no medicine there will be a major reduction in hospital waiting lists, resulting in emptier wards and a cut in the spiralling pharmaceutical bill."

Mr Davis's analysis was supported by Dr Liam Fox, who said, "All in all, these so-called problems will actually solve the biggest problem of all, ie immigration. When Britain has no fuel, no food and no medicine, who will want to come here?"

Boris Johnson also joined in the debate, saying, "Doomsday? Boomsday, more like! With no one wanting to come to Britain, we won't need a third runway at Heathrow! Bosh! Sorted! Result!"

Meanwhile, Remainers could not contain their delight at what Jacob Rees-Mogg has called "Project Fear on Speed." Said Nick Clegg, "I can't wait to be starving, ill, stuck at home and *right*!"

DIARY

MARY BEARD: JULIUS CAESAR REVEALED

Mary Beard strides into hospital delivery room, dressed in hospital scrubs.

Mary: He is the most famous – and the most notorious! – Ancient Roman of the lot. As famous in his day as Beyoncé –

Cut to footage of Beyoncé

or Posh and Becks

Cut to footage of David and Victoria Beckham

are in ours.

When his name is mentioned we think of power, victory...

Cut to footage of Donald Trump's inauguration

and betrayal!

Cut to photo of Michael Gove behind Boris Johnson

Yes, Julius Caesar changed his own world in unimaginable ways – and he's left a pretty big mark –

Cut to a splodge on the wall of a housing estate

– on ours!

In the delivery room, Mary peers over the surgeon's shoulder at a pregnant mother about to give birth.

Mary: What a lot of mums like Sally here forget when they're having a C-section is that the "C" is actually short for "Caesarian"!

That's because the procedure is named after Julius Caesar, probably the most famous – and the most notorious! – Ancient Roman of them all.

The surgeon delivers the baby and passes it to Mary

And I'm going to find out why!

Mary: More than 2,000 years after his death, Julius Caesar is still part of our everyday language.

Cut to bloke in street with rottweiller

Bloke in street: Attaboy, Caesar!

Cut to Mary pushing open the door of the Rover's Return and going up to the bar

Mary: Half a pint of your best, please, landlord!

To camera

And who can forget that mainstay of one of our best-loved soaps, Bet Lynch –

Cut to photo of Bet Lynch

– played, of course, by the fabulous JULIE Goodyear, who may not realise that her name derives from the most famous – and most notorious! – Ancient Roman of them all – JULIUS Caesar!

Mary: So who exactly WAS this man they called Caesar, long before some our our most famous soap stars jumped on the bandwagon?

Cut to Mary sitting on a bandwagon going through Rome, which stops by a statue of Caesar surrounded by tourists

Mary: Julius Caesar would be thrilled to know that we still recognise him, 2000 years later! But how much do we REALLY KNOW about THE REAL MAN?

Tourist 1: Wasn't he the one with, like, six wives?

Tourist 2: He wrote *Pride and Prejudice*, didn't he?

Tourist 3: Didn't he invent a salad?

Mary: I guess we have to start with a spoiler.

Because if there's one thing most of us remember about Caesar it was the ending. So if you don't want to know the result – look away now!

Cut to old picture of men in togas brandishing daggers

Mary: It's the 15th of March, 44 BC. Julius is on his way to work!

He gets to the senate house, and everybody's chatting and gossiping –

Cut to clip from ITV's Loose Women

Coleen Nolan: Ooh, I do love a good gossip.

Jane Moore: Well, we all do, don't we? 'Twas ever thus!

Mary: – when Julius Caesar is suddenly surrounded by 20 men. Out come their daggers –

Mary brings out a dagger, makes stabbing gestures.

Mary: – and they all start stabbing him. So what happens when you suddenly find yourself stabbed by 20 former colleagues? To find out more, I've come to the one person who really knows – Dr Hilary Jones, the medical expert from Good Morning Britain!

So, Hilary, what exactly happens when 20 people start stabbing you?

Dr Hilary Jones: Well, Mary, to put it in layman's terms, your body fills with holes and then – sadly – you die.

Mary: So, Dr Hilary, even though Julius Caesar was mega-famous, at the end of the day it didn't stop him from meeting a tragic death?

Dr Hilary Jones *(grimacing sympathetically)*: Sadly not, Mary!

Mary: And little did he know that Mark Antony was waiting in the wings.

Close up of Mary in wings

Mary: So how did a rich but frankly not A-list aristocrat get so powerful that the only solution was to kill him? Who exactly WAS Julius Caesar? I've come to Crufts to find out.

Footage of Crufts, with dogs parading around the ring

Mary: One of this country's best-loved dog foods for small and medium-sized dogs is called Caesar.

Cut to dogs being fed

But how many of these dogs tucking into Caesar classics such as Chicken and Turkey Mix and Caesar Country Kitchen Special Selection know that the man who gave it its name was the most famous – and notorious! – Ancient Roman of them all?

Spaniel owner: No, I'm pretty sure Lucky doesn't know who Caesar was. If he does, he's certainly never mentioned it.

Mary: Caesar's rise was a real masterclass in how to execute the ultimate life-changing power grab!

Cut to footage of Hitler at Nuremberg

The young Julius started off by playing the game according to the rules –

Cut to Mary playing table football in an Italian bar

Mary: Whoops! I've just let in a goal! Fair enough, guys!

Close up on Mary

But before long he was tearing up the rulebook.

Mary tears up a rule book

And refusing to play.

Mary kicks over the table

And when he left Italy for Gaul he got to lay the foundations –

Cut to Mary in high-viz jacket on a building site –

– on which all his later successes would be built. One man who can tell how he managed this is Admiral Lord West, in a funny hat.

Admiral Lord West in a funny hat: Caesar knew what he was doing, and that's vital if you want to succeed.

Mary: And, above all, he knew how to set the News Agenda. Today, that's done by 24 hour news, Twitter and other Social Media – yet Julius Caesar didn't even have his own mobile!

But he could have taught Donald Trump –

Cut to another picture of President Trump

And Kim Kardashian

Cut to picture of Kim Kardashian

And 2016 X-Factor winner Matt Terry

Cut to picture of Matt Terry

– everything there is to know about soundbites. Take this, for instance: VENI VIDI VICI – "I came, I saw, I conquered". With punchy quotes like this he truly whipped –

Cut to Mary brandishing a whip

– up national pride. Then he took the biggest gamble of his life –

Cut to Mary in Wellingtons crossing a stream

– He crossed the Rubicon – an expression that was to make him as famous today as he ever was. Here's one man who really knows – Steve Donnelly, the manager of the Rubicon Nights in Birmingham. Steve, what kind of nightclub manager would Julius Caesar have been?

Steve Donnelly: Totally brill, Mary!

Mary: So that's how Julius Caesar got to the top of the political ladder –

Cut to Mary on a step-ladder

And made him the most famous – and notorious! – Ancient Roman of them all!

As told to
CRAIG BROWN

"I'm so fed up with all the manspreading"

BORIS ESCAPES HEATHROW VOTE IN AFGHANISTAN

You are the turd runaway?

I think something's been lost in translation

Exclusive to all papers
PRESIDENT TRUMP
An Apology

IN RECENT months, in common with all other newspapers, we may have seemed to be critical of President Donald Trump for his description of London as being the most dangerous and crime-ridden city on earth, which no one in their right mind would now wish to visit.

Headlines such as "What about New York, you idiot?", "When did you last visit Los Angeles, President Moron?" and "How dare you criticise Britain when you've got Harvey Weinstein on the loose?" may have given the impression that we considered Mr Trump's comments on London to be wholly unfair, misleading and without a jot or tittle of supporting evidence.

We now realise that there was not in fact a jot or tittle of truth in our criticism of the US President's measured observations on this matter, and that London has indeed become the new murder capital of the world, where knife crime, random shootings and hammer-wielding psychopaths on mopeds are now routine occurrences in every corner of our once safe city, and that now the lawless state of London makes cities like New York and Los Angeles seem like havens of peace and order.

We apologise for any confusion our earlier coverage may have caused and wish to advise the President that if he was to come to Britain, he should avoid London at all costs and only visit one of his many golf courses in Scotland, guarded by hundreds of members of the US Marine Corps disguised as caddies.

"Don't turn over yet, babe... I'm reading that!"

Boris Johnson, the Secretary of State for Foreign and Commonwealth Affairs, writes exclusively for Private Eye

CRIPES! Old Bojo's put his size ten foot in it again! How was I to know some ghastly tittle-tattle merchant would quote me verbatim and out of context, when I'd had a few glasses of fizzington.

So, let's get this clear. I did not use the four-letter "F" word about Brexit, ie "Fail". Because a) it's not going to Fail and b) if it it does, it's not my F****!!

What I did say is that Brexit should be just like bog roll, but not namby-pamby, Andrex puppy, absorbent tissue for softies! No, it should be like the no-nonsense stuff in the khazi at Eton – hard, abrasive, painful, but gets the job done!

Ok, so this wasn't Bojo's finest rhetorical flourish and I don't want to leave you with the impression that the whole Brexit caboodle is a turd that is going down the crapper!

No. Instead I meant that we are going to be flush with success (another "F" word!) and we're all going to come out smelling of roses and not having to say "I'd give it ten years before you go in there".

Monday

Double cripes! Talking of being in the brown stuff, the Heathrow decision isn't looking too good for yours truly.

I know I said I would lie in front of the bulldozers... and I've stuck to my promise. I lied! First sign of the bulldozers and I'm hoofing it to foreign climes. In my defence, I **did** always say I was worried about the noise levels. And so now I've decided the best thing is to keep very quiet!

And thanks to Mrs May for suggesting that I take a short break during the vote.

"We need you to take your diplomatic skills abroad," said the boss, handing me a ticket.

"Where's it to?" quoth I.

"Anywhere," she said. "But how about somewhere nice and safe like Afghanistan?"

"Is it a return?" I asked, "No," she said, "With any luck, it's one way."

So off I flew and, by the time you read this, hopefully everyone will have forgotten whatever point of principle Bozza was supposedly upholding and the unfortunate bog and toilet-based imagery, and will have decided that I am essentially "a floater".

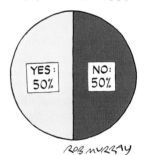

NEW POLL: IS SOCIETY DIVIDED?

YES: 50% NO: 50%

ROB MURRAY

That all-purpose Love Island article in full

I AM absolutely hooked... only watch it because my kids are obsessed, of course... more people applied than to Oxbridge, terrible indictment... ratings juggernaut... everyone watching it, well, only about one person in 30, still, very impressive... terrible toxic masculinity on display... lots of steroids... fake breasts... phwoar, all those hot bodies... I'm only watching it anthropologically, you understand... all those gleaming torsos... tiny waists but also tiny brains, they're all thick as mince... I'm only watching for the interpersonal

stories, you see... actually fascinating when you get beyond all the lithe, toned stomachs and legs from here to breakfast and biceps like five irons... cor!... wonder if Laura and Sam will get it on at any point... *(continues dribbling on for 94 pages)*

Rich survive fire at top London hotel

FIREFIGHTERS last week attended a huge fire at a luxury hotel in Central London, which saw 36 wealthy guests and 250 poorly-paid staff all evacuated safely.

The owners of the five-star Mandarin Oriental thanked the 120 firefighters and 20 engines and other emergency crews who immediately attended the scene.

The fire was dealt with successfully at the posh Knightsbridge hotel, as it wasn't started in a room by a cheap fridge-freezer – nor did the guests have to rely on a single escape route that soon fills up with smoke.

The plush hotel was also not cosmetically clad in cheap, flammable material, and the rich who were staying inside – which included the likes of Robbie Williams – were not told to "stay put" in their rooms until they burned to death.

What Facebook knows about YOU!

- Your name
- Your age
- Your gender
- Your income
- Your address
- Your interests
- Your friends
- Your resigned attitude to this

Apparently BY MIKE BARFIELD

GOING VEGAN: THE FOUR BIG 'NO'S

NO FLESH

NO EGGS

"I've been fully vegan eight weeks and I just feel so pure..." (ETC, ETC)

NO DAIRY

NO BLOODY SHUTTING UP ABOUT IT...

Daily Mail
FRIDAY, JUNE 15, 2018

THE MAIL HAILS THE 'GREATEST EDITOR OF HIS GENERATION'

by Our Media Staff **Paul Dacre**

AS he steps down from the editorship of the Daily Mail, the man who still edits the Daily Mail was first to salute himself by publishing this enormous tribute.

"Without doubt," he dictated, "Paul Dacre will go down in history, not just as the finest editor of the Daily Mail but as the finest editor of any newspaper in the history of journalism."

Who will ever forget his fearless campaigns, such as the time this morning when he flew in the face of popular opinion and bravely published a detailed and highly researched paean of praise to himself under the headline "The Mail Hails the 'Greatest Editor of his Generation'."

And let us remember that Paul Dacre was never afraid to name names – not for him anonymous winks and nudges or cowardly journalistic innuendo.

No, despite the strongest legal advice to the contrary, Paul Dacre came out and pointed the finger without hesitation, and his headline boldly pronounced for all the world to see: "Paul Dacre is the Greatest Editor of his Generation". *(That's not enough, keep going, more of this – Ed.)*

EDITOR OF DAILY MAIL RETIRES IN TRIUMPH

You see! No one is saying Leave is a bad idea now

From The Message Boards

Members of the online community respond to the major issues of the day...

Royal fan shares name

Guys! Shout out to Louis Charles Cambridge! In case you missed it, he's a 21-year-old nurse from a family of royalists who collect memorabilia, organise street parties and even create statues. His grandmother Victoria used to wave at the Queen Mother's car when she drove past on the way to the Cheltenham Gold Cup! Louis told the press: 'Colleagues kept saying, "You've got the same name as the royal baby!"' And it's true, he has! Amazingly, his mother Catherine also shares a royal name, as does father Christopher. What are the chances of that?! – *Long to reign over us*

royal babby is louis ARTHUR charles 😒 #FAIL – *bluenose*

not braggin or disrepectin but i noze a younger wiv the exak same name as prints harry he work's in camberwell mcdonalds 😎 tru story blud – *Dwayne*

iv been to that mcdonalds whats his name? – *colin*

names harry – *Dwayne*

cheers was thinkin it might be prince – *colin*

no worrys fam – *Dwayne*

I can 'Beat' this coincidence. I and my three brothers each share the name of a king AND a Beatle. – *The Walrus*

What's your name? – *PCS 3042*

George. – *The Walrus*

So your brothers are called John, James (Paul's first name) and Richard (Ringo's real name)? – *PCS 3042*

No. – *The Walrus*

You've got me stumped... – *PCS 3042*

George is my surname. I'm Steve George, and my brothers are Dave George, Sean George and Craig George. – *The Walrus*

That doesn't count. – *PCS 3042*

Says who? – *The Walrus*

You are not taking this seriously, and I refuse to discuss it further. – *PCS 3042*

george wich name is the same as your's? – *colin*

Colin, please visit Dignitas asap. I will pay. – *Jon*

cheers jon wil give it a go – *colin*

I heard 'When I'm 64' by the Beatles today and smiled at the line: 'Grandchildren on your knee / Vera, Chuck and Dave.' Then it struck me, they will have their own grandchildren by now: Shaniqua, Bakari and Mohammed. 😞 – *I pay but have no say*

theyll be on the throne soon – *shithole uk*

Time to end the disastrous democratic experiment. – *Sword of Truth*

RUSSIA WORLD CUP KICKS OFF!

Shoot!

No, I prefer Novichok

Who are you supporting?

Trump, of course!

Which is the group of death?

I haven't decided yet

FRIDAY 22 JUNE 2018 **EVENING STANDARD**

EDITOR WRITES

IT HAS come to my attention that the Evening Standard's probity has been called into question, over suggestions that this newspaper has offered 'money-can't-buy' coverage to various private firms for £500,000.

Let me assure readers – particularly any readers sipping on a delicious caramel macchiato from Starbucks, for example, or an iced one if it's too hot, yum yum – that nothing could be further from the truth. The Evening Standard has never offered positive coverage to anyone.

The Evening Standard is not for sale (partly because we give it away for free now,

because nobody was buying it). If you don't believe my claims of 100% decency and honesty, I would like to invite you to look up my record. I mean it. Just Google me. Google. That's the best search engine, I think you'll find, never mind Bing or Ask Jeeves or any of the others. Only Google delivers the results you require.

If any of these appalling claims are true, it would be a Blackrock – sorry, a black day – indeed for our reputation. Now, if you don't mind, my Uber is outside, so I have to dash very cheaply and reliably.

Yours independently,
George

Any messages Doreen?

Yes! Trevor said you are fired. Tony wants your desk and Peter says he never liked you anyway!

Dukelow

GREAT REBELLIONS OF HISTORY
BY DOMINIC GRIEVE

SPARTACIST REBELLION
70 gladiators escape from their training school, demand their freedom, and eventually agree on a modest improvement in training and working practices. Notable for the scene in which all Grieve's colleagues say "I'm not Dominic Grieve!", "I'm not Dominic Grieve either!", and are promptly nailed up.

WILLIAM WALLACE'S REVOLT
William 'Braveheart' Wallace declares war on the English lords, only to realise it's all been a misunderstanding and reaches a written agreement with them before being hanged, drawn and quartered.

THE BOSTON TEA PARTY
Outraged at taxation without representation, the colonists in America demand to pay smaller taxes, before agreeing that the British have done a lot for them and that unity is more important than turmoil.

FRENCH REVOLUTION
The people storm the Bastille and ensure a minor reduction in sentences for some prisoners, and a meaningful vote on the monarchy's excesses in future. No need for any marching, guillotines or Napoleon. Much better.

GUNPOWDER PLOT

A plot led by Grievo Fawkes threatens to blow up the Houses of Parliament and change the course of English history. But at the last minute, Grievo bravely loses his bottle and changes his mind, supporting the government while his fellow plotters look a bit silly.

OCTOBER REVOLUTION
Moscow's peasantry storm the Winter Palace, demanding Peace, Bread and Land. They leave four hours later, with a concession that if they don't get Peace, Bread and Land within twenty years they will have the right to formally lodge a complaint about it.

THAT NEW EU REFERENDUM WORDING IN FULL

Would you like to admit that you were wrong last time?

☐ YES ☐ NO

(no prizes for guessing result)

A Company Statement issued on behalf of Somerset Capital Asset Management (SCAM)

shortly to be renamed Limerick, Donegal, Tipperary and Dublin Capital Asset Management

We would advise investors in our £2 billion fund that, despite our distinguished senior partner Jacob Rees-Mogg MP's total confidence in the successful outcome of Britain's exit from the European Union, we have decided to relocate a part of our operation to the Irish Republic.

Even though Mr Rees-Mogg is sure that Brexit will undoubtedly bring Britain a period of unprecedented prosperity, vastly increasing opportunities for international investors to flock to Britain, we deem it prudent to hedge our bets by establishing a small office for SCAM above Mr Seamus O'Flaherty's widely respected bar off Molly Bloom Street in Dublin.

We believe that this safeguarding measure will serve to reassure our investors that, in the very unlikely event of the British economy totally collapsing, thanks to the very sensible approach to Brexit so eloquently advocated by our senior partner, it might turn out to be crucial to the survival of SCAM that we retain a foothold somewhere within the territories of the European Union.

We believe that our decision to relocate across the frictionless border to Ireland will serve to further reinforce the attraction of our diverse portfolio, which includes our much-acclaimed investment vehicle PUTINSCAM, which enables us to profit from the fast-expanding market in companies run by very wealthy friends of the Russian President – a man our senior partner recently described as "an appalling tyrant against whom Britain must firmly stand up at all times".

...AND IF YOU SEE ANYTHING UNUSUAL PLEASE TELL... A TRAIN!

TRUMP LAUNCHES US SPACE FORCE

"Captain's tweet, star date whatever... Spock, Uhuru, Sulu, you're all fired! Losers! Klingons great guys, so great... better than Vulcans. Our mission, to boldly go further beyond belief! Beam up some chicken wings, Scotty! Phasers to stunning blonde..."

PSYCHOLOGY

The five stages of Grieve

EXPERTS are all agreed that when you are confronted with Grieve, you go through a series of reactions which may seem extreme and contradictory but which are all part of the natural process of Grieving:

- Denial
- Anger
- Bargaining
- Depression
- Acceptance of anything Mrs May says

GOVE IN NEW BETRAYAL ROW

by Our Political Staff **Tim Shitfan**

MR Michael Gove surprised even himself last weekend when he ruthlessly stabbed himself in the back in the middle of the Chequers Brexit meeting.

Mr Gove, who has a long history of treacherous behaviour towards colleagues, was widely expected to stab Mrs May after she had foolishly trusted him with a ministerial job.

But, contrary to expectations, Gove, as the leader of the anti-May Brexit faction in Cabinet, decided to wield the knife against himself.

"It was a political master-stroke," said one observer. "Nobody saw that coming, least of all himself.

"He is now in a unique position of being fatally wounded and in a very strong position to succeed whoever is the next leader but one."

71

⚽ GREAT EXPECTATIONS ⚽

WE MUST not get over-excited by this one result. It is early days in the competition and Panama is one of the weakest teams in the World Cup. There are many challenges ahead and we should keep a hold on reality when assessing just how far our national team might progress in the tournament which WE ARE DEFINITELY GOING TO WIN FOOTBALL'S COMING HOME CRY GOD FOR ENGLAND, HARRY AND ST GEORGE IT'S HARRY XMAS FOR ENGLAND FANS KANE WE DO IT? YES WE KANE HE KANE HE SAW HE KONKERED YES! IT'S A PANAMA HAT TRICK PHEW WHAT A SCORER!?! THEY THINK IT'S ALL OVER IT IS NOW But that being said, it would be prudent to take each game as it comes, rather than allowing emotion to get the better of *(cont. p94)*

Who is the nation's favourite Harry – Harry or Harry?

In a tumultuous week for national pride, we ask the question on everyone's lips: Who is the better Harry? The England goal machine or the Wales love machine? Let the battle of the Harrys commence!

Harry Kane	Harry Windsor
Silly beard	Silly beard
Plays for country	Served country
Scores regularly	Used to score regularly
Captain's armband	Nazi armband
Number 9	Number 6 (in line)
Shoots at will	Shoots with Will
Incredibly highly paid	Quite rich anyway
No tattoo	Edinburgh Tattoo
Hoping to meet Queen	Happy to wait till Christmas
Plays for Tottenham Hotspur	Distant relative of Harry Hotspur

NEXT WEEK: Who's the nation's favourite Sterling – Raheem Sterling or Stirling Moss?

England shame

WHAT has gone wrong with English football?

Disturbing images have now emerged online showing players indulging in the kind of behaviour that is unbecoming of a sporting ambassador for our great nation.

It is hard not to feel let down by these graphic photographs of some of England's star players caught with their trousers on, as they parade shamelessly around the Hermitage Museum in St Petersburg in the early hours of the afternoon. What were they thinking?

They should be stumbling out of St Petersburg's most notorious nightclub in the early hours of the morning, with a hooker on each arm, before vomiting in the gutter, and then lying in it.

They've let down the country, the people and, above all, the media. They're bringing the ugly game into good repute!

What is the world coming to? Some of them have double-barrelled names for God's sake: Loftus-Cheek, Alexander-Arnold?! One of them's even called Fabian! They think it's all over – it is now!

England stars make an exhibition of themselves

A Doctor Writes

AS A doctor, I'm often asked "Doctor, have I got World Cup fever?"

The simple answer is "Yes, you have". What happens is that the patient experiences a range of symptoms, including increased heart rate, palpitations, profuse sweating and a feeling of irrational optimism, followed by a sense of impending doom.

This is perfectly normal and sufferers from World Cup Fever or Baddiel's Syndrome, as it is often colloquially known, may be found running through the streets, pulling their shirts over their heads and introducing an extra syllable into the word "England".

There are few known remedies for World Cup Fever or Lineker's Complaint, as it is also known, but a massive intake of alcohol is no longer thought to be an effective antidote, in fact quite the opposite.

Also, watching repeats of Midsomer Murders on ITV4 is no longer recommended by public health officials, as the fever is aurally transmitted and it is almost inevitable that you'll still be infected by the cries of fellow sufferers next door or in the pub down the road.

Be warned, World Cup Fever, or *julius rimetus etiam gleamingensis* to give it the full medical term, is still extremely contagious and merely having caught it previously (say, in 1966 or 1990) does not make you immune from any fresh outbreak. It can strike anyone, even those who've shown no previous interest in football, talking of which, is that the time? We've missed the kick-off, COME ON INGERLAND! No, we can do it, we really can! This time, I'm daring to hope! Get in there, you beauty! Penalty, ref, for fuck's sake! Fucking hell, Southgate, you muppet, you don't know what you're doing!

© A Doctor, 2018.

"There needs to be a law against upshirting!"

Exclusive to all newspapers

IS THIS THE BEST-RUN WORLD CUP EVER?

by Our Football Staff **E.I. Adidas** and **Nike Cohen**

THE entire world has gazed in awe at the astonishing efficiency with which Russia has organised the most orderly and trouble-free sporting tournament in living memory.

Who has not been filled with admiration at the sight of football fans of all nations peacefully enjoying a festival of sport without a hint of the old familiar scenes of drunkenness, hooliganism and violence which have so often disfigured previous international sporting competitions?

How on earth has Russia managed to pull off such a triumph for law and order and the proper spirit of friendly sporting harmony?

The key is surely the admirable principle which governs the way in which President Putin rules his great country.

Not only does he provide the necessary funding for sport itself, so that the world admires those magnificent stadiums in remote locations that will never be used again. But even more impressive, he has made sure that Russia's police force is sufficiently well-manned, well-trained, well-disciplined and well-armed to leave any potential troublemakers, whether sporting, religious, political or otherwise, in no doubt that stepping out of line will immediately result in arrest, deportation or sudden, unexplained death.

Truly, the way President Putin has used the football World Cup to show the world how these things should be done is a lesson the rest of the world could heed.

Let us give credit where it is due. He has staged the most impressive international sporting occasion since the late Herr Hitler's Berlin Olympics in 1936.

"When the tournament's finished, all this will be converted into a henge"

British economy 'set to boom'

■ There were predictions today of a sudden turnaround in Britain's ailing retail sector, as it experienced a waistcoat boom.

"Sales of waistcoats in the last few weeks are already up over 5,000 percent and that trend shows no sign of abating," said one retail analyst. "On many of Britain's high streets today there is nothing else on sale apart from waistcoats."

It is thought that, on current predictions, by the end of the week, every single man in Britain will look like a snooker player up to his neck in gambling debts in a Guy Ritchie film.

"Ugh! Footie fans"

TV HIGHLIGHTS

Top Fear

Sunday 8pm
BBC2

Matt Le Blanc and the boys review all the latest motor manufacturer threats to leave the country post-Brexit. Who will be fastest? Jaguar or BMW? It's the battle of the supercars! High-octane European thrills as The Stig outlines Britain's position on the impact of the government's Third Way proposals for petrolheads!

Eye rating *Probably the scariest programme… in the world!*

ME AND MY SPOON

WORLD EXCLUSIVE

MR MARKLE (MEGHAN'S DAD)

Do you have a favourite spoon?

No, but Prince Harry told me his favourite spoon was a good old-fashioned British spoon.

Did he mention European spoons?

Not exactly, but my understanding was he wouldn't give them drawer space, if you know what I mean!

But what about *your* spoon preferences?

Well, you know, Prince Harry called me up to shoot the breeze about spoons before the wedding, as you do, and I told him I'm no admirer of Trump spoons.

And why is that?

The President only likes American spoons made out of 100 percent US steel. If we're honest, the guy is spoonist! But then Harry says to me in confidence, just between the two of us, "Meghan's dad! You should give Trump spoons a chance. Maybe they'll turn out OK." He's young, he'll learn!

Have spoons played an important role in your life?

The most important thing in life spoonwise is to treat other folks with respect. As I said to Prince Harry, "Never raise a spoon to my daughter." And, you know, I believe he's an English gentleman and he knows how to treat a lady in matters of the spoon.

OK, quick spoon question – dessert or soup?

Soup for me, I'm always in it, particularly when I told Meghan I couldn't attend the wedding. She wept and I don't think it was with joy! No siree.

Do you worry that talking about Royal Spoon secrets might be embarrassing?

No, I think you are doing a very good job, Piers.

NEXT WEEK: *Arron Banks, Me and My Banks.*

HEIR OF SORROWS
A Short Story Special

by Dame Sylvie Krin, author of *Duchess of Hearts* & *You're Never Too Old*

THE STORY SO FAR: Charles is attending the christening of his newest grandchild. Now read on…

POP! went the champagne cork, as Prince William's friend, Guy Silly, opened yet another bottle of what he insisted on calling "Fizzington".

"Time to wet the baby's head! Again!" shouted Silly, as he filled the glasses of the assembled young people. Who were they all? Charles wondered. Was that Araminta Cutzem-Jetsam-Flotsam ? And was she talking to the younger Ricketson-Smythe? Tarquin, was it? Or Crispin? Or was it Dave?

Charles worried that he could no long remember all the names. There were Kate's tribe, the Middleclassingtons, busily advertising their new range of christening party balloons and "Baptise-me-Kwik" hats. He remembered them, of course… er… Mrs and her husband Mr and the sister Poppa and beardy the boy… thingie Middleclassington… Come to think of it, what was the baby's name? Louis Theroux Arthur Daley Telegraph… no, that couldn't be it. Charles! That was the name! And a very good one too.

"Cheer up, Chazza! You look like the ghost at the feast," chided his consort, Camilla, as she attempted to give the newly christened baby Louis a quick vape "to keep him quiet". Charles tried to smile as Kate hurriedly took the baby away and gave him to her mother.

"That's the whole damned problem. I am like a ghost, drifting around as if I was invisible."

"Whoops ! Sorry, Gramps, didn't see you there," shouted Trinny Leggy-Toffington, as she bumped into Charles and accidentally showered him with vintage Bullinger Grand Cru.

"Who was that clumsy young personage?" grumbled Charles, thinking that, after all, he was not just some old bloke making up the numbers, but the Prince of Wales, Earl of Chester, Duke of Cornwall, Duke of Rothmans, Baron of Hardup, Lord of the Dance and many, many other titles that deserved a little respect.

"In fact, when you think about it, she really is… well, there's only one word for it… appalling!"

As Charles moved towards the buffet with its range of stylishly named "Font Food" from the Middleclassington Christening Collection, he overheard a conversation drifting over from the Harry 'n' Megan set.

"I think he's behaving very well, all things considered," gushed an actress from some programme on Netprofit, or one of those box-set channels he didn't watch.

"Defo!" agreed an Old Etonian – who may have been Darius Cholmondeley-Foode-Banks or possibly Charles' godson, Pongo Money-Bagges. "No tantrums. No crying. No throwing his toys out of the pram."

"Yes, indeedy doody," soothed the unmistakeable empathetic Californian voice of the newly-wed Princess Markle of Sparkle. "I think Prince Charles is on top form."

"Oh yah," agreed Prince Harry. "Megs is totes right. Pater is playing a blinder."

The room seemed to spin around Charles's weary head. What was worse? Being ignored or patronised ? Either way, it really was…

"APPALLING," said the heir to the throne, as he relaxed in his Whitehouse & Mortimer Victorian cast-iron bath. "There's no other word to describe that Trump fellow. Don't you agree, Sir Alan?"

Charles's aide-de-high-camp, Sir Alan Fitztightly, murmured his agreement, as he poured into the water a double dose of Duchy Originals Organic Tar and Feather Bath Balm.

"His record on LGBTQ issues is very poor, sire."

"Yes, that and the Pussy Riot thingie and, of course, his views on climate change… I mean, there's no way I could meet a monster like that."

"So very unlike your friend the Emir of Sharia Araby, with his liberal views on so many things…"

"Yes, thank you, Sir Alan." Charles cut off the factotum royale in much the same manner as his friend the Emir was wrongly being accused of cutting off the feet of women drivers or whatever it was… Fake news, as someone had so rightly put it…

"I mean, when you think about it, this Trump man is a great big baby, spoilt and petulant, out of touch with the real world, with ridiculous views on subjects he knows nothing about…"

What sounded like a snort emerged from the elegant proboscis of the official Squeezer of the Royal Toothpaste.

"Sorry, sire. Hayfever."

"Well, I am not going to meet him. Mater can do it."

"Perhaps, sire, constitutionally it should be up to the Prime Minister of the day to decide these things and…"

"Fiddlesticks! I shan't meet him and that's that! Now leave me in peace – I have urgent business to attend."

As Sir Alan shimmied out of the room, he glanced back to see that His Royal Liegelord was engaged in a re-enactment of the launch of the *Sir David Attenborough*, using the plastic model ship given to him by the Polar Exploration Society.

"I name this ship *Boaty Mc*… what was it again?"

Charles's mind whirled like the flows and eddies of his bathwater, as the miniature *Boaty McBoatface* sank to the bottom of the tub.

To be continued…

DOUBTS CAST OVER 'GENERATION SENSIBLE'

We drink less, we smoke less, we trust Jeremy Corbyn

HIGH STREET DEAD

That list of possible suspects in full

1 Amazon
2 Ocado
3 Deliveroo
4 Vladimir Putin
   (Salisbury only)

mummy, what's a shop?

snizelda

SINCE YOU'RE AWAKE, I'LL HAVE A MUG OF TEA AND A BACON ROLL

K.J.Lamb

Prince Charmless

Jeremy Corbyn WRITES

HELLO! It's me again. And we know the thing that is most occupying my mind. Gardening. And once I've finished fertilising my carrots, the next thing most occupying my mind is Brexit.

Like you, I've been appalled at the mess Theresa May is making. As I said in my amazing performance in the Commons this Monday: she's had two years, and the Tories can't even agree on a single policy on Brexit. I mean, how hard can it be? We in the Labour party have had exactly the same amount of time and we've got dozens of Brexit policies! We've already discarded the Norway, Switzerland, and Canada models and I think Keir's nudging towards the Cuba model (no membership of the Customs Union or Common Market, but we hope to sell revolutionary t-shirts with my face on to tourists).

And now with the embarrassing resignation of David Davis and the appointment of some jumped up junior nobody Dominic Raab, it just brings it home as to how badly Brexit is being managed.

When I see the chaos she is making, one question comes up time and time again. Why oh why, didn't she do the sensible and obvious thing and appoint ME Brexit secretary?

It would solve all her problems. I've got grey hair and I've got as much worth ethic and attention to detail as David Davis. I'm also as loyal. I would make an excellent Brexit secretary because I believe in the project much more than Davis or anyone else left in the cabinet. After all, Tory ministers are only supporting Brexit for perks and a chance at the top job, but I'm happy to shred my reputation and the electoral chances of my party to get some taste of that sweet Brexity goodness.

Of course, she also missed a trick by not appointing me Foreign Secretary. If she wants continuity, then I'm your man. Like Boris, I'm an expert at ignoring uncomfortable questions about Iran, and if I was in the FO, failing to answer questions about Iran would be what I would be best at – I've certainly had the practice!

So Theresa, come on, get a grip on Brexit pronto or I will have no choice but to stop whipping my MPs to mindlessly support everything you do. Okay, that would be a little hasty! But if Raab has to resign in the next few weeks, you know where I am (Islington Allotments, plot number 23A. I'm the old, bearded man who looks slightly less like a party leader than the other old, bearded men).
Cheerio!

DAVIS QUITS

I'm leaving on very bad terms... so no surprises there!

BORIS QUITS TOO

I'm doing a U-turd

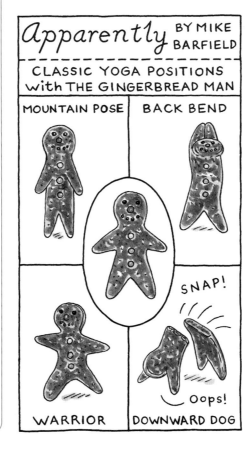

Apparently BY MIKE BARFIELD

CLASSIC YOGA POSITIONS with THE GINGERBREAD MAN

MOUNTAIN POSE

BACK BEND

WARRIOR

SNAP!

Oops!

DOWNWARD DOG

Why the Trump Balloon is an Outrage

by **Isabel Oakeshottinfoot**

WHATEVER you think about Donald Trump's politics, the decision by Sadiq Khan to allow a balloon caricature of the president to be flown above London during his visit is indefensible .

It is childish, pathetic and, above all, offensive to a visiting head of state who is, after all, the leader of our oldest ally and a democratically elected politician.

A far more mature and responsible idea would be to fly an enormous gas-filled balloon caricature of Sadiq Khan. Ok, so he is the Mayor of London democratically elected with a huge mandate but who cares?

You don't think I'm going to be consistent, do you? Heard the one about Cameron and the pig? Vote Leave! Can I have some money please?

© Isabel Footshott 2018.

That Non-State Dinner Menu In Full

Duck à la Extremely Orange

Poulet in a jus of chlorine

*Caged veal
(separated from parents, lightly beaten)*

Grabbed poussin

Far-Aged beef with Brown Nose Sauce

Poutine

*Please Please Please
(can we have a trade deal) Pudding*

– ❉ –

*Desserts:
Muslim Ban-ana bread with Walls ice cream*

(That's enough menu. Ed.)

TRUMP VISIT

What an offensive, inflated, gas-filled blimp!

...and so is this balloon

PRESIDENT'S 'HIGHEST LEVEL OF SPECIAL' RELATIONSHIP

I think I've pulled!

AMERICAN TOURISTS VISIT ANTIQUE EMPORIUM

Nice old chest!

You are very rude man, Donald, zis is Queen not porn star

BBC IN HELICOPTER DRAMA

THERE was a spectacular scoop for BBC News yesterday as, acting on a tip-off from legal insiders, a camera crew captured the moment that the BBC lost its privacy case against Cliff Richard.

As the BBC's Head of News emerged from the court and tried to get into a taxi, a specially commissioned helicopter swooped down from the sky to beam images of the BBC's shame and embarrassment into viewers' homes.

The BBC sought to justify the unwelcome intrusion into the life of its Head of News, saying, "The BBC is a high-profile national treasure that we strongly suspect of behaving very badly with young-looking, innocent pop stars. Only by hiring a helicopter to cover the news, can we expose the pointlessness of hiring helicopters to cover the news."

Asked whether he would now be sacked for his intrusive coverage of the Head of News' embarrassment, the news editor responsible replied, "You'll have to ask my boss, the Head of News, but at the moment she's too busy not resigning."

The BBC's legal correspondent said, "This is a dark day for free speech. It's essential that the press be allowed to name suspects, such as"

'Turdy McTurdface' gets thumbs down

THE name "Turdy McTurdface", approved by 97.6 percent of the population as a new name for Mr Boris Johnson, has been rejected by the Ministry of Names as being "an inappropriate nomenclature for one who has held, until recently, a senior office of State". *(Reuters)*

● *Full story p94*

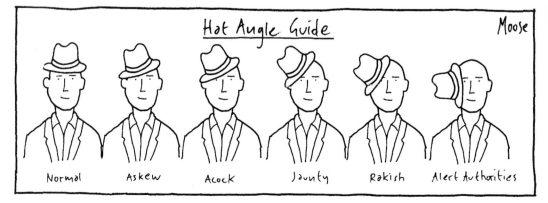

Hot Angle Guide — Moose

Normal   Askew   Acock   Jaunty   Rakish   Alert Authorities

DIARY

GERMAINE GREER

For Christ's SAKE, first you have to answer the question as to whether women should be persuaded to live their whole lives in a state of chemical dependency, like everybody knows Queen Elizabeth II has done AND CONTINUES TO DO because let's face it no one in their right mind would go grandstanding around the world with that look-at-me expression on her face morning, noon and night at the age of 98 or whatever and WHAT'S MORE dressed in the most ABOMINABLE clothes if it wasn't for the WELL KNOWN FACT that the poor old thing is force-fed Prozac and who-knows-how-many barbiturates by the prime minister who AS EVERYBODY KNOWS comes with a variety of state-of-the-art syringes and a huge box of pills and tables to Buckingham Palace for their weekly so-called friendly meetings friendly my foot (!) which all goes to show that like her best friend MICHAEL JACKSON who she would sometimes speak to three, four times a day the Queen is under the direct control of the big bosses of the male-dominated multinational corporations who basically mastermind all her actions and engagements every single one of them which is why OF COURSE she wore that hideous phlegm-coloured dress when she went to Canada last year, which was her way of telling the Canadians to do what the US government says or the boot would be firmly put right in because why else would Ant McPartlin have split so publicly from his so-called wife Lisa Armstrong thus jeopardising his long-term partnership with Dec who by the way I've always found truly DETESTABLE particularly over his refusal to voice ONE SINGLE WORD against the disgraceful behaviour of Xi Jinping of China who by encouraging the cultivation of noxious GM crops has ensured that men ALL OVER THE WORLD will continue to treat women as secondary to their first love which is IT GOES WITHOUT SAYING dogs particularly spaniels poodles labradors and bull-terriers not to mention the WATER BUFFALO which AS WE ALL KNOW has always been a breed of dog, but there's been one hell of a cover-up about it, and so now the water-buffalo has had to suffer the EXTRAORDINARY indignity of re-classification which is why you'll never find a water buffalo in the final at Crufts not in a million years just because Peter FUCKING Purves who LET'S FACE IT masterminds the whole event from a secret underground office outside Geneva, refuses POINT BLANK to accept the fact that for centuries the water buffalo has been one of the world's best-loved household pets I mean I grew up with a water buffalo sitting on my lap and my best friend at school had a baby with a water buffalo which I might add was VERY frowned-upon in those days but what do you know in the rigidly male-dominated society of Australia at that time they considered that this beautiful creature this half-woman, half-buffalo could be put to good use so BEING MEN they forcibly removed her from her mother and from what I hear she was DOOMED to spend the rest of her days chained to a typewriter specially adapted with extra-big keys to accommodate her half-hands half-hooves writing diatribes DICTATED BY PETER PURVES against the role of the water buffalo in society which is why WIND FARMS which by the way caused the great conflagration on Saddleworth Moor the other day IN FACT are the greatest threat to our society since THE TEDDY BEAR which and this is COMMON KNOWLEDGE just look it up if you don't believe me was introduced by that FASCIST monster Theodore Roosevelt as a way of FORCIBLY SENTIMENTALISING an entire nation so that when ADOLF HITLER came along in the early Thirties we'd all be too weedy and fucking SOPPY to stand up to him instead sobbing over our disgusting furry bears with their brains made out of stuffing so now we're all meant to worship GEORGE fucking CLOONEY with his disgraceful NESPRESSO MACHINES which as we all know are taking over the world they're not for making coffee DON'T MAKE ME LAUGH but for drugging the weak minded into submission to a consumerist culture to such a revolting extent that when Love Island's Megan shared a steamy kiss with Wes leaving Laura watching on in absolute HORROR she had obviously somehow convinced herself through imbibing TEN GALLONS of Nespresso that this would be a career-changing move and now what's she left with yeah too right she's left with her character in tatters and by the way that bikini thong does her no favours I mean what was she thinking she's got an ARSE on her the SIZE of New Zealand and frankly I fear for her because it leaves her open to obnoxious sexist cat-calls from the brutalised males who make up 95 percent of the viewers and who LET'S FACE IT have absolutely ZERO respect for women's inalienable right not to be judged on their bodies even if like TV's Holly WILLOUGHBY they insist on flaunting their pumped-up little bodies – and surely I can't be the only one who's spotted a massive acreage of CELLULITE on her impossibly flubbery legs though there's not much she can do about that so let's just give her a break, guys and FOR CHRISSAKE there's a wider point to be made here about immigration in the European Union because FOR CRYING OUT LOUD anyone with half a brain knows that Angela Merkel is in the pay of the Chinese just like Celine Dion before her and that's why Germany are out of the World FUCKING Cup so it all BOILS DOWN to what I said on Radio 5 Live yesterday morning and for which I might add I was ROUNDLY CHASTISED which is that the world would be VASTLY improved if the British army OR WHAT REMAINS OF IT was sent in to eliminate all household cats with a single shot through the eyes because LET'S FACE IT they are just taking up all essential oxygen with all that shitting and miaowing because as I plan to say in an unguarded moment at the Cheltenham so-called literary festival the cat-loving Martin Luther King was the racist to end all racists let's not beat around the bush he was a one hundred percent white man who spent three hours at the start of each day blacking up to get on television and by the way Mary Berry is WELL KNOWN to be one of the most spiteful people alive and what's more she can't cook for toffee and that's your fucking lot send me my fee by return £2,500 for eight minutes plus VAT for Chrissake.

As told to
CRAIG BROWN

I'm not dumping it,
I'm renting it out on Airbnb

any ideas for the opening of
our new flagship store?

closing down sales
normally get the punters in?

I'm arresting you for doing some data
related thing that's way too complicated
for me to get my head around

is that the office? yeah, the sun's just
gone in, does it still count as a day off?

Hundreds of Tory MPs throw hats in ring to succeed Mrs May

by Our Entire Political Staff
(many of whom are thinking of standing themselves, even though they are not MPs)

WESTMINSTER was rocked to its foundations yesterday when it became clear that every single Tory MP has now decided that he or she would make an infinitely better job of being prime minister than the "utterly useless" Theresa May.

It was impossible yesterday to find a single member of the parliamentary party who had not set up banks of telephones in rented rooms all over Westminster, creating their campaign HQ for the forthcoming leadership contest.

Said one leading obscure junior backbencher, who asked to remain anonymous (Hugh Hee, MP for Little Knownsley East), "I don't know why all these other idiots think they are remotely fitted to become PM. Surely everyone can see that only I have the flair and charisma to rescue Britain from the disaster Mrs May has inflicted upon it.

"As a typical Tory party activist (my wife) said to me only this morning, "You did a fantastic job as Parliamentary Under-Secretary for Digital Paperclips for over three months. You are clearly the front-runner."

Liz Truss is 15 and Jacob Rees-Mogg is 97.

That 2nd referendum
How it will look
Would you like a second referendum?

YES ☐   NO ☐

That 3rd referendum
How it will look
If the second referendum didn't go your way, would you like another referendum to revert back to the position before the first referendum?

YES ☐   NO ☐

That 94th referendum
How it will look
Do you think it is the job of elected politicians in a parliamentary democracy to sort these things out because that is the whole point of their existence?

YES ☐   YES ☐

Vince Cable slammed for missing vote

LIB DEM leader Vince Cable came under fire today after missing a key vote that would have brought down the Conservatives.

Asked why he missed the key vote that would have brought down the Conservatives, Mr Cable, who is known to be keen to bring down the Conservatives, replied, "I couldn't attend the key vote that would have brought down the Conservatives, as I was busy attending a key meeting about how to bring down the Conservatives."

No Lib Dem MPs were available for comment as they were at a key meeting about how to bring down Vince Cable. *(Rotters)*

That Donald Trump Foreign Policy Playbook In Full

Step 1	Threaten nuclear apocalypse and very tough action via Twitter
Step 2	Claim you are willing to meet horrible dictator of Russia/North Korea/Iran etc
Step 3	Meet horrible dictator, say nothing to challenge him at press conference
Step 4	Point out how impressive horrible dictator is at running trains on time
Step 5	Strongly imply you wish America was a bit more like horrible dictatorship
Step 6	Claim enormous progress on highly complex issues after 20 minutes of talks
Step 7	Go home
Step 8	Nothing changes
Step 9	Rogue nation continues developing nuclear weapons/abusing human rights
Step 10	Repeat

EU Negotiations Latest

"Add something to this..."

The Secret DIARY OF SIR JOHN MAJOR KG aged 77¾

Sunday

I was not surprised, as the country's leading and most respected elder statesman, to have received a call from the Andrew Marr Show (after William Hague, Michael Portillo, Ann Widdecombe and someone off Sherlock had all said no), asking if I would appear on this Sunday's edition to discuss Brexit.

I told them I would in no small measure be delighted to appear. I replaced the handset on the phone and turned to my wife, Norman.

"Theresa May could learn a lot from what I achieved facing down the bastards in my party over Europe, couldn't she, Norman?"

"Yes, dear," she uttered. "I'm sure she'll be equally capable of ushering Labour into power for a generation, darling," she continued, passing me the milk.

"No... no... no," I said. "I meant, how I would highlight the dangers of tossing aside the benefits of a union which was responsible for many happy memories over the years. Oh yes."

Sadly, I never got to discover if Norman agreed, as at that precise moment she clumsily upended a bowl of cornflakes over my head and then she refilled the bowl and did it a second time. She really is getting quite clumsy these days.

I continued, soggily, "It will also give me a chance to argue for a second referendum. Because everyone deserves a second chance after making a disastrous decision which involved lies and deception, don't they, Norman?"

Once again, Norman didn't answer, as almost inexplicably for the third time that morning she stumbled and upended a bowl of cornflakes over my head, leaving me not inconsiderably damp.

"You're wetter than Rees-Mogg," chuckled Norman, in that teasing way of hers.

NEW WAVE OF MIGRANTS ARRIVES

Everyone in Europe wants to throw us out

It's like being Angela Merkel

AQUARIUS

Let's Parlez Franglais!

Numéro 94

Le Nouveau Minister de Brexit visite à Bruxelles

Michel Barnier: Ah, bienvenu, Monsieur Raab! Vous êtes le nouveau kid sur le bloc!

Dominic Raab *(pour c'est him)*: Oui, et je suis très different than Monsieur Davis.

Michel Barnier: C'est vrai. Vous êtes ici on time, pour starters!

Dominic Raab: Et ce n'est pas plus de Monsieur Nice-Guy!

Michel Barnier: Monsieur Davis n'était pas un Nice Guy. Il était un Demi-Asleep-Guy.

Dominic Raab: C'est tout le history et l'eau under le pont. Je commence avec un brand nouveau, clean sheet de papier.

Michel Barnier: Ah, vous avez la même sheet de papier que Monsieur Davis had après deux ans de négociations!

(Entre Jean-Claude Druncker, un petit peu le worse pour wear.)

Jean-Claude Druncker: Mon Dieu! David, vous avez changé beaucoup! Vous avez perdu weight et aussi perdu tout votre hair! Et vous êtes awake!

Michel Barnier: Non, non, Jean-Claude. C'est Dominic, le nouveau patsy avec le job impossible.

Jean-Claude Druncker: Oui, c'est un mission even plus impossible que le mission impossible de Tom Voyage Maritime.

Dominic Raab: Non, Madame May a un plan de Chequers fantastique et je suis l'homme to faire it happen.

Jean-Claude Druncker: Hahaha! Avez-vous been drinking?

Dominic Raab: Non! C'est huit heures dans le morning.

Jean-Claude Druncker: Huit heures? Vraiment? C'est temps pour un stiff one.

Michel Barnier: Careful, Jean-Claude, vous might collapse.

Jean-Claude Druncker: Juste comme les Brexit négociations! Hahaha! Bienvenu aboard, Monsieur Crab.

Dominic Raab: Actuellement, perhaps je will have ça boisson, après tout!

(Continue à 2094...)

© *Kilomètres Kington.*

I THINK I'LL GO TO SLEEP NOW....

-ROSS-

Life before the internet

Nursery Times

·········· Friday, Once-upon-a-time ··········

DISH AND SPOON TO SPLIT

by Our Showbiz Staff **Twinkle Star**

THERE was surprise and disappointment in Nurseryland at the news that the nation's favourite dish had split with her younger spoon, only two years after they had run away together.

The dish, Cheryl Tweedydum, made her name as part of the all-dish group, Crockery Aloud, who were similar but not quite as famous as the chart-topping Spice Rack: Spicy, Ginger, Salty, Peppery and Turmeric.

The dish left the group to marry top footballer Old King Cole, but he proved too merry an old soul and fiddled about too much, so she left him.

She then got married again and changed her name to Cheryl Rumpelstiltskin-Dish, which nobody could guess right.

"This time it's forever and a day," she said, but unfortunately it was just a day. Finally, she ran into the spoon on a talent show called The Eggs Factor, hosted by Simple Simon Cowell, in which contestants had to make an omelette.

The dish and the spoon soon became inseparable, despite their age gap, and this time they promised that there would be a fairytale ending. But there wasn't. No one lived happily ever after, and the couple asked for people to respect their publicity.

JUMBLIES TURNED AWAY FROM ITALY

by Our Migrant Staff **Edward Fear**

A SIEVELOAD of Jumblies has been turned away from Italy as they seek to escape from their land far away far away.

The Prime Minister of Italy, having been voted in on a wave of anti-Jumblie feeling, said "We're not rejecting them because their heads are green and their hands are blue, oh no. It's just we've had enough Jumblies now, it's time for some other countries to take their share of Jumblies."

He continued, "If they're looking for a better life, why can't they go to the Torrible Zone and the hills of the Chankly Bore, or better still, Spain?"

Friday, Aug 10th 2018

Mail Online | Jan Moir

Look who's still desperately seeking attention at 60!

YES THAT'S RIGHT IT'S ME, JAN MOIR. Isn't it time I stepped aside to allow some younger hackettes into the spotlight?

No way! Just as I did when she turned 30, 40 and 50, I'm still hogging all the column inches penning half-arsed hatchet jobs about why Madonna should age gracefully.

IT'S MUCH TOO HOT TO WRITE THIS ARTICLE

by Our Sweating Correspondent **Phil Space**

GOODNESS, IT'S HOT!

Yes, it's very warm indeed in this office, and the statistics are telling me it's definitely time I was off on holiday, am I allowed to go yet? *(No. Ed.)* Right, fine then. I suppose I could tell you about the technical definition of a heatwave, but it's frankly a bit too hot to look it up. No, I think the real thing we all need to bear in mind is that the air-conditioning's broken, which seems to me to be a human rights violation, yet I'll have to write about how all those archaeological sites are appearing through the scorched yellow grass, or how it's actually much cooler in Spain, it'd be nice to be in Spain now, are you absolutely sure I can't go there? *(This is hopeless. You're fired. Ed.)* Oh, thank God for that, right, I'm off to Spain, bye everyone!

THOSE HEATWAVE DAYS OF THE WEEK IN FULL

Melting	Monday
Tropical	Tuesday
White-Hot	Wednesday
Thermonuclear	Thursday
Furnace	Friday
Stormy	Saturday
Sodden	Sunday
Melting	Monday

Etc...

"We're joined now by a leading climatologist. So, how do we account for the peculiar weather: Brexit or Trump?"

POPULAR SONGS REVISITED NO 94

The Sun Has Got His Hat On
Hip! Hip! Hip! Hooray!
The Sun Has Got His Hat On
Roughly 30 Dead Today!
(This is appalling, Ed.)

"Yes... my husband burns easily too"

MAMMA MAY!
— HERE WE GO AGAIN —
THE FEEL-BAD EVENT OF THE SUMMER

FEATURING: Knowing Me, Knowing EU
● **Gimme! Gimme! Gimme! A Plan After Midnight** ● **S.O.S.**

The Just So Predictable Stories

by Mr Kipling (who writes exceedingly good tales)

Number 94: **THE CROCODILE**

ONCE upon a time, in a land bordered by the great grey-green, greasy Limpopo River, all set about with fever trees, there lived a crocodile, who was the second most important animal in the jungle of Zimbabwe, after the dreaded Mugabe monster.

And when the people got rid of the evil Mugabe, the crocodile said, "I'll take over instead". The people weren't too sure about that, as the crocodile was a crocodile, so they said, "Since you are a crocodile, perhaps we should have a general election to see if there's a more suitable candidate to lead us through a period of democratic change." And the crocodile said, "Sure, no problem, I'll organise the election, just leave it to me." And so the election was held and the crocodile campaigned on the promise that he wasn't really a crocodile but he was a cute kitten.

And after the votes were in, the crocodile counted them himself and told the people, "Guess what, people, I've won!" and started behaving like a crocodile and not a kitten. And the people were surprised and raised mild objections, at which point the crocodile killed and ate up everybody who didn't agree with him, because he was quite obviously a crocodile.

The moral of the story is:
A leopard may change its spots, but a crocodile never changes its government.

Vote Leave disputes Electoral Commission ruling

by Our Political Staff
Tim Shipshape

After the Electoral Commission issued its verdict, finding that Vote Leave had broken spending rules during the EU referendum, the leaders of Vote Leave refused to accept the result.

"We want a second ruling, we don't accept this one," said Vote Leave spokesman, Mr Arron Bankroll. "We don't like it, it's not fair".

However, the electoral commission stood by its rulings, saying, "What bit of it don't you understand, losers?! Suck it up!"

LESSONS FROM HISTORY Number 94
The Corn Laws

IN THE 19th century the Tories made a most dreadful mistake under the leadership of the much reviled Prime Minister and First Lord of the Treasury, Theresa Peel.

Mrs Peel, whose only agricultural experience was running through a field of wheat, was concerned about the situation in Ireland and decided that the only way of solving the potato famine problem was to lower the price of corn.

This proved unpopular with traditional Tory supporters, particularly those amongst the landed gentry in Somerset, who quite reasonably preferred to make lots of money rather than save lives. The situation ended in tragedy, with the Tory party splitting, losing office, and failing to regain power for many years. I believe some Irish folk came to an unfortunate end as well.

Mrs Peel, however, unaccountably put the good of the country above the good of the party, and for that she was never forgiven and remained the most hated Tory Prime Minister until Sir Robert May took over in 2016.

At the time, the only figure to emerge with any credit was the charismatic dandy and orator with the fashionable clothes, Mr Benjamin Dismogg, who captured the mood of the nation in several TV appearances by opposing Mrs Peel and, later in his career, making a heroic U-turn, accepting the necessity of free trade rather than protectionism.

The lessons are quite clear. If you're going to run a hedge fund, move to Ireland and make sure your principles don't get in the way of making money. That, and don't let Rees-Mogg anywhere near a history book.

Venus de Lilo

UNIVERSAL CREDIT
Case studies show extent of problem

At first, Mr I.D.S. thought Universal Credit sounded like a brilliant idea. Unfortunately, because nobody had given him relevant training nor shown him how to properly spend his money, he wasted all his available cash on computers that didn't work, meaning that he lost all credibility. He has now lost his job and any sense of purpose in life. He is depressed, embittered, and unlikely to find any meaningful work.

Ms E. McV. has clung on to her job so far. Sadly, her experience of Universal Credit has been just as bad: thanks to terrible delays and arrears, E. McV. was tragically forced to mislead her colleagues and pretend she was doing well at her work, when an independent report revealed how badly she was doing. Now she's seen as a liability and widely mistrusted by her colleagues. In some ways, E. McV. is suffering just as much as families going without benefits for five weeks on end.

BORIS IN TALKS WITH DEVIL

by Our Political Correspondent **Christopher Marlowe**

THE former Foreign Secretary Mr Boris Johnson has surprised observers by admitting that he has been having "serious conversations" with Beelzebub, a seasoned political operator who calls himself "a disruptor" and who is known for his extreme views and his hatred of the status quo.

Beelzebub, or Steve as he is manifesting himself at this moment in human history, has been working mostly in America recently but has now decided to bring his own version of alternative ethical philosophy, ("alt-right" or simply "wrong") to Europe.

There was initially some confidence that there was no one in Britain desperate enough to summon Beelzebub (apart from Nigel Farage, obviously) but recent news stories have confirmed that Boris has indeed sunk that low and Beelzebub in return has gone on the record to endorse Mr Johnson and has declared that "Boris Johnson would be the best prime minister for Britain".

There are worries, however, that the cost of this support may be rather high, ie Mr. Johnson's soul, and that, were Boris to sell this to the devil in exchange for supreme power, there might be terrible repercussions.

"We have always known that Boris was ambitious but for him to end up working for Satan would be disappointing," said a Conservative insider. "We did not mind him being arrogant and deceitful and vain but for him to be actively evil might put off possible Tory voters".

Mr Faustus Johnson, however, remained unworried. "Who says you can't serve God and Bannon?"

PROJECT FEAR MK2 'MOCKED'

BREXITEERS have mocked as "ludicrous" some of the outlandish scare stories regarding the no-deal Brexit, which they claimed are being used to try and scare the public into opposing Brexit.

Amongst the far-fetched "disaster scenarios" they have claimed won't happen:

■ Supermarkets running out of fresh food within days

■ Planes grounded

■ Food rationing being reintroduced

■ Lifesaving medicines being unavailable

■ Army on the streets to maintain order

■ Jacob Rees-Mogg elected prime minister

Apple becomes first billion excuses company

■ There was joy today in Silicon Valley as Apple narrowly beat Google to be the world's first billion excuses company.

"Apple came up with their billionth excuse for why it was only paying £349 tax in the UK on profits of $29bn, a whole three minutes before Google's billionth excuse, that paying tax would result in it not making as much profit, was released."

Silicon Valley said it expected that in the years to come hundreds more tech companies will join Apple and Google in the "billion excuses" club.

Omega 3 'Does Work'

■ Herbal nutritionists have rejected a major study by the respected Cochrane Library, which has found that taking Omega 3 supplements does not improve health by maintaining heart function.

Practitioners at the world-famous HerbalBolloques Institute say their studies have found taking expensive Omega 3 fish oil capsules increases levels of gullibility in its patients.

"Nine out of ten of our patients taking Omega 3 on a daily basis increased their levels of gullibility by as much as 500%."

Jeremy Corbyn WRITES

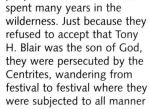

HELLO! It's me again. Well, once again I've been forced to intervene over a sinister strain of prejudice that infects our Labour party like a cancer. I don't know where it comes from but it needs to stop now.

The prejudice against me, which I like to call Anti-Jeremism, is held by a small number of well-meaning but misguided Labour members who have this visceral knee jerk reaction to the state of Jezrael. It's anti-Jeremism that threatens the whole Labour party and it must cease.

I keep having to say this, sadly, so I will say it again, if you criticise me in any way, even in the abstract, you are criticising Jezzahs (both Orthodox and Diane Abbott) and will be expelled from the party forthwith.

Don't forget that my people, the tribe of Jezzah, spent many years in the wilderness. Just because they refused to accept that Tony H. Blair was the son of God, they were persecuted by the Centrites, wandering from festival to festival where they were subjected to all manner of indignities, including Billy Bragg.

Eventually, they found a home on the Mill Bank; a small place to call their very own, and they immediately set about peacefully spreading themselves around and removing everyone who didn't share their faith, as is the prerogative of any persecuted people.

And it's because of this tiny historical fact that they are so hated. Just look at the anti-Jeremism displayed by Margaret Hodge only the other day. Such ingratitude! You'd have thought that she would be honoured that our new anti-Semitism guidelines were named after her, being as they are a complete Hodge-Podge. But now she has clearly broken the guidelines as shown below.

1. Anti-Jeremism is a certain perception of Jez which may be expressed as stereotyping him as an ignorant, blinkered old man who can't really see he ever does anything wrong.

2. This sentiment is usually expressed by annoying Jewish people.

3. Goodbye.

There you go. It's there in black and white.

Anyway, can't sit around here typing. I'm a busy party leader. Got to organise Momentum's annual jolly to Stratford. I know it's the *Merchant of Venice* again, but you never get tired of the classics!

Cheerio!

amazon PROFIT

TAX

amazin

Why Amazon is terrified of social unrest By Jeff Bezos

1. If there's a post-Brexit atmosphere of fear and mistrust then neighbour will turn on neighbour

2. This means that when the package is delivered to number 33 there will be nobody at number 35 willing to take it in

3. Entire Amazon business plan is shot

4. Er... That's it.

THE BREXIT HIGHWAY CODE

Caution: Elderly voting in referendum

Oh dear

Dover, 2020

OUTRAGE AS ELDERLY WOMAN IS REFUSED DIVORCE

by Our Legal Staff **Joshua Rosenbeard**

BRITAIN was astonished yesterday by an unprecedented legal ruling that a woman who for years has been seeking a divorce would not be permitted to escape from her unsatisfactory marriage.

The woman, a Mrs Theresa May, has long been attempting to win a divorce from her partner, known for legal reasons only as "EU", on the grounds of "unreasonable behaviour" going back 40 years.

However, after listening for many months to her attempts to justify her case, the judge, Mr Justice Barnier, ruled that she had failed to produce "any convincing evidence which could lead to a satisfactory resolution of her difficulties".

He told her, "I'm afraid the fact that you are clearly a very unhappy and confused woman does not in itself prove that your long-term partner has behaved unreasonably.

"It appears that for 40 years you have gone along quite happily with everything your partner said and did, and frankly it is a bit late now for you to make out that you were always miserable.

"As I have repeatedly tried to explain to you and your, I fear, wholly incompetent legal team headed by Mr Davis," the judge concluded, "the law is the law.

"Whether you understand it or not, that remains the case. Which is why there is no way I can allow this marriage to end until March next year, when you will have to accept whatever terms the court shall decide.

"I can only suggest that you go home to your sad little island and cry your eyes out, thinking of the unnecessary distress you have inflicted on your patient and long-suffering partner."

Mrs May is 61.

Middle-class cocaine users to blame

by Our Drugs Staff
Charlie Everywhere

Britain's most senior police officer, Metropolitan police commissioner Cressida Dick, has attacked middle-class cocaine users, saying not only do they fuel the rise in gang crime, but even worse, fuel the rise in really tedious dinner party conversations.

"For too long people have remained silent about the link between a dreary middle-aged businessman snorting a line after the tiramisu and then talking non-stop bollocks for the next hour about the screenplay he's always wanted to write, because he's actually a very creative person," said Cressida.

"And the same goes for his wife, describing in detail after snorting up a large line of white powder, how wonderful her three adorable children are, what a struggle it was getting them into the local grammar, how useless the nanny is, and how, even now in her mid-40s, she still fits into the wedding dress she wore 15 years ago.

"Anyone who has been on the receiving end of one of these coke-fuelled narcissistic rants knows only too well the pain and suffering they bring and why we need to stop them," said Cressida.

*"Not only does he have the hypocrisy to snort coke, he's using a **plastic straw**!"*

DIARY

JOHN CLEESE

This country! I mean, REALLY! And then people ask me why I'm upping sticks and getting the hell out of here – whoops, pardon the old lingo, Brigadier Swizzlestick (Mrs), as we used to say in the Pythons!

And while we're on the subject of the Pythons. It might be of some mild interest to one or two people – *memo to all you cloth-eared imbeciles out there, I'm now partaking of IRONY, in the unlikely chance you know the meaning of that word!* – when I reveal that the BBC has consistently failed to repeat Monty Python over a period of many years, which quite clearly means that they are terrified that it'll show up just how UTTERLY PATHETIC most of their new comedy is, or so I'm reliably informed, as I never watch it myself.

Oh, and by the way, doesn't it strike you as rather extraordinary TO SAY THE LEAST that Donald Trump – that's President Donald Trump to you and I – has NOT ONCE mentioned Monty Python OR ANYTHING TO DO WITH THE PYTHONS – in a single one of his public statements for over three years. And that's a fact that has been consistently verified by a number of university professors. All of which strongly suggests to me that Trump's in the pay of Murdoch, who has been consistently against the Pythons ever since we had the ABSOLUTE BLOODY NERVE to introduce the British public to the essentially subversive message of satire – remember satire?! – back in the good old 1960s. And if there's one thing Murdoch and Hitler and Stalin and the rest of 'em absolutely can't stand, it's satire. Hence, the outright ban on Python that the BBC's been enforcing these past umpteen years.

And then they ask me why I'm leaving the country!

I'm frankly so disappointed with so much about this country. Take Brexit, for instance. I mean, really! As it happens, I voted to leave but no one – NOT A SINGLE PERSON – bothered to make it clear that this would entail us leaving the Common Market or the EEC or the GCSE or whatever it likes to call itself these days. The powers that be – no doubt guided by Dacre and Murdoch – kept us ENTIRELY IN THE DARK about what that vote would mean. So inevitably, when it came to filling in the ballot form, I was one of many millions who were led to believe that ticking the box marked LEAVE would mean that we would stay in Europe and ticking REMAIN meant we wanted to leave. So we were totally and utterly hoodwinked by the louts and imbeciles who are meant to be serving us. And they still persist in calling it a democracy! Unbelievable!

And this country used to pride itself on its sense of humour. Sense of humour! HA! Remember that? It's fascinating, really. Nowadays, whenever I crack a joke – and you may have noticed, I'm rather well-known for my jokes – NOT A SINGLE PERSON laughs. Not one. Instead, they just sit there utterly stony-faced. Whereas, in the old days they'd literally HOWL with laughter.

Just the other day, I performed in front of 2000 or so people, and I cracked some splendid jokes about my ex-wife – about what an unpleasant, money-grabbing, blood-sucking, crap-spewing tart she turned out to be – and do you know what? Not so much as a TITTER! Very sadly, the British people have totally lost their sense of humour, and all in the space of a generation. If it wasn't so depressing, it would be very funny. But they still wouldn't laugh, because they've been taught not to by the Daily Mail and successive right-wing governments.

I was reading a survey conducted by an eminent university professor of 793 people in South Dakota – and that's a very, very sizeable sample, by anyone's reckoning – and it turns out that an overwhelming 56% of them believe that – and I quote – "the United Kingdom is not as funny as it used to be". Pretty devastating, I think you'll agree. And young people are the worst. Whenever I talk young British men and women through classic Python sketches like the Ministry of Silly Walks or the Parrot sketch they barely even BOTHER TO SMILE. Too lazy. Too frightened. It's frankly terrible what's happened to this country. And that's why I'm packing my bags and "vamoosing", as we used to say in the Royal Ballet Corps of Little Snodsbury! HA!

It's official. To demonstrate our total and utter disgust at the moral, political and social DEPRAVITY of "Great" Britain – and, ladies and gents, please take note of the inverted commas around the adjective "Great" – my wife and I are moving to the delightful Caribbean island of Nevis. Unlike this GODAWFUL country, the relationship between the races is absolutely superb in Nevis. The last time we were there, those excellent folk served us the most delicious seafood dishes, and first-class wine, and they were full of smiles and were only too eager to please, with none of the surly, shifty resentment one has sadly come to expect from their counterparts in Britain.

You see, it's the lying and the ignorance and the utter TRIVIALITY I object to about this country. Very few people over here have THE SLIGHTEST IDEA what is going on in the world, because Murdoch and Dacre want to keep them in ignorance, just like Stalin used to do, so that they don't storm the barricades of the BBC and demand proper repeats of Python. And it means they don't realise that Vladimir Putin is a regular presenter on Fox News, or they're never told about the recent survey of 725 people by a very experienced professor at Wolverhampton University which concluded that a staggering 67% of them couldn't name the Brexit secretary, whoever he or she may be. And if you quote the classic Python Cheese Shop sketch at any length to anyone under the age of 40 these days, well, they give you a look of BLANK INCOMPREHENSION.

I mean, really. This country!

As told to
CRAIG BROWN

*"If it is any consolation, the public loves your dress...
It's just flying off the shelves"*

More tales from the Mister Men
Mr Markle

POOR Mr Markle is feeling left out. His daughter, Little Miss Markle, has changed her name to The Duchess of Sussex and is refusing to speak to him.

But Mr Markle will speak to anyone – Mr Pressman, Mr Tellyman, even Mr Moron from Good Morning Britain!

Silly old Mr Markle. He thinks they're his friends, so he tells them all about how sad he is and how much he hates Little Miss Markle's snooty new family. But this only makes Little Miss Markle even crosser, and even more determined not to talk to Mr Markle ever again.

What a sad story. How can it possibly end?

Mr Cheeky says, "Don't go to Paris and stay at the Ritz, Mr Markle, and don't get in that car, just in case."

Labour and Tories attack each other for racism

by Our Political Staff
Harry Pot and **Martin Kettle**

The two main political parties last week devoted their entire energies to accusing each other of harbouring extremist bigots in their ranks and allowing senior figures in the party to pander to their prejudices.

Said a Tory spokesman, "What we can clearly see here is a political party which is doing nothing to discourage some very unpleasant attitudes in its membership... but enough about uo... or... did you ooo thooo pictures of Corbyn at the terrorist funeral? Jeremy Corbyn? Jeremy Cor-bin-Laden, more like!"

A Labour spokesman immediately responded, saying, "I have never seen a party more riven with prejudice and religious intolerance. And the Tories are even worse! Did you see that story about Boris and his Facebook followers? Facebook? Fascistbook, more like!"

Meanwhile, the leader of the Liberal Party said something which nobody could be bothered to report.

A-Level Standards Questioned

by Our Education Staff
Joy Jumping

THIS year's A-Level results have prompted renewed debate amongst experts as to the exact levels attained by students.

Whilst the government claims that pupils are reaching new heights, experts are more sceptical and are suggesting that, in fact, the pupils are **not** jumping as high as they did previously.

Said one, "The photographs have been adjusted to make it look as though nothing has changed."

Said another, "We don't know exactly where the ground is, so they could be jumping six inches or three feet. We just can't tell."

A spokesman for the Education

Department said, "Every year, people try to undermine all the hard work that the pupils put into their jumping. Their achievement of getting onto the front page of all papers should not be belittled by fogeyish critics, claiming that jumping was much harder in their day."

TRUMP TELLS WORLD 'DON'T TRUST SUPERMAN'

by Our White House Staff
Colonel Huckabee Sanders

PRESIDENT Trump today lashed out at the US's number one superhero, describing him as un-American, unpatriotic and not to be trusted.

"I've read a lot about this guy. Okay, I haven't read anything, but I saw the film on TV, and you're not going to believe this but Superman is actually a journalist. That's right! He's a disgusting person. Clark Kent – dishonest purveyor of fake news at the failing Daily Planet! He says he's got super-powered vision to see through me. But everyone can do that! What a phoney!"

The president then went on to remove Superman's security clearance. The superhero will no longer be able to fly around in US airspace saving those in danger.

Trump then tweeted, "The guy's a flake. Even lies about his identity to his girlfriend. Lying to a woman – who would do that?! Is it a bird? Is it a plane? No, it's an enemy of the people. #Loserman."

Go back to where you came from

"We tweak the grades awarded to the lowered marks in the harder exam required by the revised syllabus to ensure that the standard remains the same"

Emma Bighead

Every August I am reminded of how well I did in my A-Levels and how there was a picture of me on the front page of the newspaper.

Nowadays, I only make page 94, but it is still a chance to remind everyone that I got three As (which was the top grade then, obviously) and was blonde, which was all down to my hard work and being cleverer than everyone else.

Did I mention that I was blonde (still am!) and got three As? Because I did and it was very exciting and important and I was even photographed for the front page of the newspaper.

You'd think being so clever, I might dress this column up a bit, so it doesn't come across as unremitting boastfulness, but what's the point? I can't escape the fact that I got three As with hardly any revision, and none of those excellent grades was for modesty.

© *Emma Blonde-Barnet.*

Corbyn denies anti-semantic accusation

by Our German Linguistic Staff
Herr Split

LABOUR leader Jeremy Corbyn found himself at the centre of a new storm, loosely based on the previous storm, over whether or not he had taken part in a wreath-laying ceremony in a cemetery containing the graves of former Palestinian terrorists.

Mr Corbyn said, "I was present but I was not involved." He continued, "My use of this phrase makes it clear that I am not anti-semantic, I have the highest regard for semantics. I hope this unclarifies the situation."

Corbyn denies anti-cemeteryism

LABOUR leader Jeremy Corbyn has found himself at the centre of yet another storm, loosely based on the previous new storm in which his denial of attending terrorist wreath-laying led to accusations of anti-cemeteryism.

"This is a grave charge," said Mr Corbyn, "and as a man who likes to dig a big hole for himself, I am offended by this charge. I was actually honouring all the people who'd ever been buried in this cemetery and in all the other cemeteries all over the world.

"It was my personal and heartfelt tribute to all of the 108 billion people who have died since the beginning of time when Cain sent Abel to an early grave – oh God, they weren't Jewish, were they?! Help!"

BRITAIN'S OLYMPIC LEGACY

Pity it's Munich 1972

POPE'S MESSAGE FOR IRELAND

I promise you, no more cover-ups

fringe
FIVE TO WATCH

■ Fascist comedian **Adrian Hitler** is sick of the boring, Lefty, politically correct comedy that has overrun the Fringe, and his show, *Kill The Weak*, refreshingly subverts the typical tropes of most so-called "comedians"!
★ *As recommended by the Spectator.*

■ **Jenny Flange** is not afraid to do a stand-up comedy show all about mental illness, depression, anxiety, OCD and bipolar disorder. There are no jokes at all, as that would be inappropriate.
★ *As recommended by the Guardian.*

■ Visiting American comedian **TrukNutz**, star of the late-night American TV circuit, is turning up to do just one night in an 8,000-seat venue and will charge £35 a pop for the privilege.
★ *Recommended by anyone who's anyone.*

■ A well-established comedian can't be arsed to turn up and do a month of shows, so he's written a play instead. Very dull.
★ *Not really recommended by anyone.*

■ Student improv troupe **GigglePrix** have a boundless enthusiasm and *joie de vivre* which will make you truly appreciate life outside the theatre after the show ends.
★ *Recommended by their mothers.*

FUNNIEST JOKE ON THE FRINGE
This year's top Edinburgh Zingers!

1. "I lost my job in the shoe shop. They gave me the boot"
– *Ivor Laff, The Laff Show, The Lead Balloon, Venue No. 94.*

2. "I got a new job at a tailor's doing adjustments to trousers. That was a bit of a turn up"
– *Anna Nutherone, The Brexit-in-the-Title Show, The Underpant, Venue No. 994.*

3. "Why do they call it Brexit? It should be 'Brixit' because we are all scared about what's going to happen. See what I did there?"
– *Cliff Edge, The Something-to-do-with-Trump Show, The Left Luggage Office, Waverley Station, Venue No. 9,9994.*

(As chosen by the Comedy Channel Dave-Ja-View-UK-Plus-One)

House prices crash to 2% higher than they were

THE housing market has been completely routed in recent months, with prices tumbling down to a staggering 2% higher than they were this time last year.

"This is disastrous," said one industry expert. "Imagine having a housing market where houses get very slightly more expensive, instead of one with huge bucketing gains every year so Foxtons can buy all their staff Maseratis. It's an absolute disaster."

Another industry insider said, "If prices keep falling at this rate – by which I mean getting higher by lower amounts than they used to – young people will still not be able to afford somewhere decent to live, so that's some consolation for people who already own their own homes."

Trump 'unable to attend McCain funeral'

DONALD TRUMP has revealed he only didn't attend Senator John McCain's funeral alongside former Presidents George W. Bush and Barack Obama after receiving medical advice.

"I was all ready to sign up to do a reading when my doctor diagnosed a bone spur," the President told reporters in the Oval Office. "That ruled me out totally of participating in the service.

"Such a great shame," he said, before remembering to add "Ow!"

He continued, "For all our differences, I'd really liked to have seen McCain in a wooden box, hopefully being prodded with sticks by some of his Viet Cong torturers for old times' sake."

Exclusive to all US newspapers and copied by all UK newspapers and the BBC

POETRY CORNER

**In Memoriam
John McCain, US Senator and Presidential candidate**

So. Farewell
Then John McCain,
The last true
American hero.

You were the
Epitome of everything
That made America
Truly great.

Honest, decent,
Courageous, dedicated to
Public service,
Unfailingly courteous,
A beacon of civilised
Values who was
Universally revered
Across the world.

Have you got the
Message yet?
Ie, how completely
Unlike he was in
Every way to
Someone else we
Do not even need
To name.

   Edwin Jefferson Thribburger,
    Poet-in-Residence at the
    Liberal Studies Faculty,
   University of New Dworkin.

DANGER CHILDREN

RGJ

YOU'RE FUCKED!

HMG

B.

**Government's
No-Deal Brexit Advice**

A Doctor Writes

AS A doctor, I'm often asked, "Doctor, do you think Laura Kuenssberg is pretty or should she wear a bag over her head?" The simple answer is "How dare you, you sexist, misogynist bastard, take that."

What then happens is that the doctor throws a punch at the other doctor before they engage in a fully blown punch-up or *Pugilisticus Medicus Intoxicatissimus*. Symptoms of this condition include severe thirst, irritability and a referral to the medical practitioners' tribunal.

If you are suffering from *Kuenssberg's Syndrome,* do not seek medical advice, as it may lead to a blow to the head and an appearance in the Daily Telegraph.

© A Doctor 2018

The issue that's got everyone in Britain talking...

SHOULD THE BURK BE ALLOWED IN PUBLIC?

by Our Political Staff NIQAB ROBINSON

IT's the biggest political question confronting Britain today: should we permit Boris Johnson to continue poisoning the well of our public debate?

Critics of the Burk insist that every time he opens his mouth, he makes Britain a less civilised and rational country to live in.

They are calling for Johnson's mouth to be kept firmly covered at all times. They argue that it is perfectly permissible for him to show his eyes, but they insist that under no circumstances should he be allowed to show his mouth in public.

Defenders of the Burk explain that Mr Johnson should be free to say anything he likes, in order to keep himself in the public eye, as he prepares to mount his campaign to replace Mrs May as prime minister.

It is, they argue, a matter of deep personal faith to Boris that he is the only person fit to lead the country, and he will do anything to further this cause.

That is why he must be allowed to dress up his overriding ambition in any way he chooses, such as his posing as a defender of free speech, providing that it is his own speech that must be defended.

It would be outrageous, say his supporters, to cover up the Burk's mouth in public, since it is the only way he can continue to put across his core message to the people of Britain – namely, that he will do anything to gain supreme power, in order to rescue Britain from the catastrophe created by the fanatical belief system of himself and his allies.

WHAT DO YOU THINK?

Should Britain

Ban the Burk? ☐

Allow the Burk in public places, such as No.10 Downing Street? ☐

ECB PROBES CRICKET DRINKING CULTURE

by Our Cricket Staff the late **Christopher Martini-Jenkins**, **John Drinkarlott**, **Henry Blowtothehead** and **Jonathan Aaaargnew**

THE England and Wales Cricket Board is to investigate what is widely seen as a problem with over-consumption of alcohol amongst its elite cricketers.

One of the first areas it's going to investigate is a list of fielding positions, found in the pocket of Ben Stokes' whites:

Those Fielding Positions In Full

- First Sip
- Second Sip
- Third Sip
- Gulpy
- Shorts Leg
- Long Legless
- Pint
- Cover Pint
- Whisky Keeper

A spokesman for the cricketers' bible denied that there is any drink problem. "We at Wisden's Armagnac have seen little evidence of any pervasive drinking culture, though there have been some changes of terminology." His list included:

- **Out** used to mean no longer batting, but now means no longer conscious.

- The **Drinks Interval** now takes place at 3 o'clock in the morning and consists not of lemon barley water but beer, vodka and Jägerbombs.

- **Bouncer** was formerly a term for intimidatory bowling, but is now the subject of intimidatory abuse outside nightclub.

- **Duck** used to apply to a batsman's score of nought, and is now advice for anyone approached by Ben Stokes outside Mbargo nightclub.

- **Chucking** which used to be a frowned-upon bowling action, is now a vomiting action at close of doors.

- **Collapse** which used to denote batting failure, now means failure to stand upright.

On other pages

UNIVERSITY CHALLENGE

EDWARDS | BARTRAM-TWISELL | ST.JOHN-THORPE | BIG TITS

BOYCE

Top public school in 'initiation rite' scandal

by Our Education Staff Wackford Squeers

THE headmaster of St Cakes, the famous independent Midlands school (motto: *Quis Paget Entrat*) has admitted that boys "hitting each other with cricket bats" is completely unacceptable.

Mr R.G.J. Kipling told reporters, "Of course we can't have pupils administering corporal punishment to each other under the guise of some sort of initiation ceremony."

He continued, "No. If anyone is thrashing, caning or beating new boys for no reason, then it should be members of staff, not their contemporaries.

"I do apologise to any parents who paid good money, £23,000 per term (tuition fees not included), on the understanding that their children would be beaten by myself, not Perkins Major from the lower sixth."

Mr Kipling makes exceedingly good canes. *(Surely "cakes"? Ed.)*

Lines written on the investigation of the former first minister of Scotland for alleged sexual harassment

'Twas in the year two thousand and eighteen
That Alex Salmond was questioned as to where his hands had been,
And whether he had been somewhat remiss
In the particular colleagues he had chosen to kiss.
The former First Minister admitted he'd been flirty,
Though strenuously denied he'd done anything dirty.
Indeed he said he had no reason for guilt
As to what went on (or not) beneath his kilt.
But the leader of his party, cool Nicola Sturgeon,
Cut poor Alex off, like a limb by a surgeon.
So Alex said I'll fight ye all in court
For saying I've done things I did'na ought
And to underline the unfairness of the case against me
I hereby resign my life-long membership of the SNP.
And in a fit of righteous but canny entrepreneurial rage
He set up an online legal-defence crowdfunding page.
But what would the outcome of the investigation be?
Would he be disgraced or would he walk free?
Of only one thing can we be entirely sure,
We'll see yon Alex one day on that shiny *Strictly Come Dancing* dance floor.

© *William McGonnagal 1867*

From the Daily Torygraph

A Tragic Day in Our Island Story

CHARLES BOORE

It may have escaped the notice of the ordinary reader, but I cannot resist drawing your attention to a truly remarkable historical landmark.

For the first time ever, Britain today has a Conservative cabinet without a single member having been educated at Eton.

Is it any wonder that this extraordinary moment should coincide exactly with our country falling apart in every respect?

It is widely agreed that Eton is the finest school not only in Britain, but in the entire world.

Even today, it still provides many of the most capable and influential figures in British Public Life. One thinks of the present Archbishop of Canterbury, the actor Mr Edward Redmayne, the future King of England, the Duke of Cambridge, and his hugely popular brother, the Duke of Sussex.

Indeed, I have to admit that the distinguished list includes myself.

It is surely a matter of considerable national significance that a school which over the centuries has produced so many of our country's most eminent luminaries should now be lamentably ignored as a source of the inspired national leadership that we so desperately lack.

One thinks of great statesmen, from Pitt the Younger to David Cameron, or towering wartime leaders, from the Duke of Wellington to Sir Anthony Eden, of great adventurers, from Captain Hook to Bear Grylls, or masters of the English language, from George Orwell to, dare I say it, myself.

Can it really be true that today there is no one fit to take on the mantle of all these outstanding figures who were there when their country needed them?

No. There is one obvious candidate who must surely now step forward to command our loyalty, as we face the gravest challenge Britain has known since the Repeal of the... *(surely the Battle of Agincourt? Ed.)*

I shall not insult your intelligence (even if you did not have the benefit of the world's finest education) by naming the saviour of the nation I have in mind. However, I shall give you a clue.

The OE I have in mind does not have the initials J. R-M (although he would indeed be an excellent choice for the role).

Obviously, the one I have in mind rejoices in those other only too familiar initials A.B. de P.J.

● *Editor's note. What the hell is this about? If you mean Boris, you should just say so, you Old Etonian twit.*

RUSSIANS PROTEST AGAINST PUTIN PENSION REFORMS

Our Timid Leaders Can Learn From Strongmen

by Our Times Columnist
Clare Monger

I hear disparagement of strong leaders these days, but these critics fail to understand that there is an attraction for decisive leadership. Like them or not, they get things done. Trump, Putin, Erdogan and Duterte... Yes, they might be a little controversial, but people who hold their hankies to their noses don't understand that these strongmen are the future and surely they are better than leaders who just talk, make promises and don't deliver.

This is why the decision by the BBC not to include the Daleks in the next season of Doctor Who is wrong.

The Daleks have a clear, easy-to-understand pledge to exterminate everyone who is different from them and they carry out their campaign pledges to the letter, and you have to respect that. They get things done, as long as that thing is exterminate, exterminate or even exterminate.

Unpalatable as Daleks may seem to liberal elites, they are surely preferable to Doctor Who, with her mushy ideas of nice outcomes that are "good" for people. Good for whom? Only those who want to live in peace, and who listens to them anymore?

I, for one, would welcome being subjugated by crazed homicidal half-robots as long they weren't Obama or *(cont. on Twitter, which is the only reason for this column existing)*

EXCLUSIVE TO ALL RIGHT-WING PAPERS

Why oh why does the pound keep betraying Britain?

Enemy of the people

WHY is it that every time it looks as though UK Plc is booming, with unemployment at an all-time low, productivity soaring and the recent heatwaves resulting in record sales for those shops still left in our streets, the pound decides to take another nose dive?

Doesn't the pound realise that its primary duty is to stay strong and support Britain?

Just as Theresa May is battling to bring her negotiations with Brussels to a triumphant conclusion, the pound yet again attempts to undermine her efforts by treacherously plummeting to a new low.

We say it is time for the pound to stop talking itself down. It must learn to grow up and become a responsible patriotic currency, like the Chinese renmimbi, the Russian rouble and the Turkish lira.

British Citizenship Test

THOSE THERESA MAY DANCES IN FULL

- The Liam Foxtrot
- The Can't-Can't
- The Limbo (bending over backwards)
- The Out of Timewarp
- Down in the Poll-dance
- The Hokey Cokey (in, out, in, out, Brexit all about)
- The Military One-Step (after defence cuts)
- Toe the Line dance
- The EU Twerking Time Directive
  (You're fired. Ed)
- The Macaron(a)
- The Reel (no Reel is better than a bad Reel)
  (You're fired again. Ed)

How the Daily Mail covered the Theresa May dance

How embarrassing for our Prime Minister to humiliate herself in such a way before the world's media, by desperately attempting to prove her street credibility and show herself in some way "down with the kids", by participating in an excruciating display of sexagenarian gyrations which made you fear for a hip operation. This was surely more suitable for Christmas Day in a Nursing Home, rather than an official visit to drum up trade with friendly nations. It is sadly the latest of her failures to come across as a genuine human being rather than a robotic automaton. Shame on you, Mrs May!

How the Daily Mail would have covered the Theresa May dance if she hadn't joined in

How stuck up can you get? The Prime Minister has once again demonstrated that she's a robotic automaton unable to come across as a genuine human being. By refusing to get "down with the kids" and show a modicum of street credibility, she embarrassed herself and the nation in front of the world's media. What we wanted was an exhilarating display of sexagenarian gyrations, the kind that might have made us fear for a hip operation. Instead, she remained aloof and clung to what she imagined was Prime Ministerial dignity, but was in fact just another failure in a long list. Shame on you, Mrs May!

OLD LEFTIE WHO DOESN'T SUPPORT PARTY DRIVEN OUT OF LABOUR SHOCK

by Our Political Staff **Mo Mentum** and **Owen Goal**

THERE was widespread astonishment throughout the Labour party last night when maverick, grey-haired, left-wing veteran Frank Field was allowed to quit the party.

Why isn't he being made leader instead?" asked one bewildered Corbynite.

"He is everything we admire in the new Labour party," said another. "He is even a Brexiteer, though he could keep a bit more quiet about it, but honestly, he ticks all the boxes."

Said another, "And his name – Field – it even sounds like an allotment. I'm totally confused by this principled, disloyal, old-fashioned, difficult, committed troublemaker."

All three then burst into song: *"Oh, Frank Field!"*.

Jeremy Corbyn is 94.

HOW THE OTHER PAPERS COVERED THE THERESA MAY AFRICAN DANCE

Who do you think you are, luv, Prince bleedin' Charles?

It takes years of Royal training to learn to boogie to the bongos. When it comes to embarrassing jigging about in a tropical suit, next time – leave it to the heir to the throne

The Guardian

In a disgraceful display of cultural appropriation, our Prime Minister proved that once again she is an Imperial racist to rival Cecil Rhodes and Rudyard Kipling.

It was worse than Al Jolson blacking up, or Laurence Olivier playing Othello; attempting an ethnic dance was at the same time patronising and rude, a brutally offensive insult to our shameful history of colonialism, slavery and genocide.

FINANCIAL TIMES

It is regrettable that a single error of judgement by the Prime Minister has led to a collapse in the value of the pound and a run on the shares in the FTSE one-hundred.

Confidence in the British economy suffered a huge shock halfway through her first shuffle and has not recovered since.

DAILY EXPRESS

Diana would have danced much better – if only she hadn't been murdered by the Duke of Edinburgh, begging the question: why is winter here so soon?

Fingers Crossed Rail

HS2 project 'still on track'

THE Government has insisted it's still committed to the £156b HS2 rail project, despite announcing a 12-month delay, pointing out it had recently begun the compulsory purchase of large amounts of land with long grass.

"Once we have acquired sufficient quantities of long grass," said a spokesman for the Department of Transport, "then we can commence phase two, which will involve kicking HS2 into it. We're still confident HS2 will cut the journey time between London and the North, provided you own a car and have a wee before you leave home, so you don't have to stop at the motorway services."

(Rotters)

7,000 POLICE CUT

Goodbye, Goodbye, Goodbye

NEW AFRICAN AGREEMENT

Theresa May has hailed as a "breakthrough" a new trade agreement with Africa.

"I received a very important email last night which is a turning point in trade relations between our two countries.

"All I have to do is give the account number of the Bank of England to this Nigerian prince, and he will transfer me these diamonds he and his brother discovered in this mine."

The Nigerian prince in question has emailed his delight. "I have spent many years trying to find someone in the UK this credulous, and now I have.

"I had a good feeling about Theresa when she brought Liam Fox back into her cabinet."

IT'S BODYGUARD MANIA!
ARSE IN POLITICAL DRAMA

TV

Reality

Chris Evans joins Virgin Radio

VIRGIN RADIO says it has every confidence Chris Evans can recapture the magic of his time at the station in the early 2000s, after he sensationally quit the Radio 2 Breakfast Show to rejoin Virgin.

"Obviously, we're slightly worried about just how professional and not at all drunk Chris Evans is these days," said a Virgin Radio spokesman, heading down the off licence for some vodka and cheap cider.

"But we're confident that after a few marathon sessions down the pub with Danny Baker, Chris can recapture the magic of old by not turning up to present his breakfast show for weeks on end before we sack him.

"We've even got Billie Piper on standby at the Elvis Wedding Chapel in Vegas to seal the deal."

POETRY CORNER

**In Memoriam
VS Naipaul**

So. Farewell
Then VS Naipaul.

Many great writers
Only use their
First two initials, ie

TS Eliot
AA Milne
CS Lewis
WH Auden
JK Rowling
HG Wells
JD Salinger
Etc.

EJ Thribb (17½)

FOREHEAD WRINKLES LINKED TO HEART ATTACKS

If I were you, I'd pop into Sickbay

HOW TV'S 'BODYGUARD' IS REALLY BRILLIANT AND IS BASED ON ME

Me!

by all female former home sexretaries

As a female former home secretary, I watched *Bodyguard* and was impressed by the level of accuracy in the research.

Not only were the day-to-day machinations of a senior Cabinet Minister represented in an authoritative and accurate way, but the dealings with the police and security services also rang true. The daily briefings, the high-level Cobra meetings, the difficulties with colleagues, the rumours of potential leadership crises all had a convincing verisimilitude.

I really recognised myself in Keeley Hawes' character. Steely, determined, clever, yet fantastically attractive, totally fit, and obviously fancied rotten by all the men around me. Especially the hunky bodyguards who couldn't wait to get me in a room and rip off my trousers and…
© *Amber Rude and Jacqui Smutt*

Viewers complain that 'Bodyguard' is unrealistic

AFTER the first episode of BBC1's new flagship drama aired, there was widespread criticism of *Bodyguard* for its lack of realism.

"I think when the hero sensed something was wrong on the train, based on nothing but a hunch, found a suicide bomber in the first toilet he knocked on and convinced her to leave the train single-handed without getting shot… it just lost it for me," said one viewer on Twitter.

"Why was there a functioning toilet door? I completely lost my suspension of disbelief. Why didn't it fall open and show the suicide bomber sitting on the toilet holding it shut with her foot?"

"Those female marksmen running through the train with their big guns was just nonsense," said another angry viewer on Twitter.

"It would not happen. They would have fallen over all the commuters unable to get a seat, squatting in the aisles."

"I was most offended when the Euston train was pulled off into a siding because there was a suicide bomber on board," added a Mr C. Grayling yesterday.

"Having a train stop for an actual reason instead of no reason at all makes a nonsense of everything I work for, and insults our hard-working, privatised rail shareholders."

Look darling! There's a man eating shark!

Dukelow

GLENDA SLAGG

Fleet Street's Hacky Sharp!! Geddit?!?!?

■ VANITY FAIR?!?! Vanity Phwoar, more like?!!? All those handsome hunks in scarlet tunics!!?? I'd tip my bonnet at them any day?!? Makepeace Thackeray?!? Makelove Thackeray, more like!!?!?! *(You've done this. Ed.)* So what's wrong with being a flirty, ambitious, good-time gal who's going to sleep her way to the top, eh, Mr Editor??!? Just saying!!?!? *(This is brilliant. You are definitely not fired. Ed.)*

■ BODYGUARD??!? I'll guard his body!?!?! Richard Madden, I'm talking about, stoopid!?!? He's the hunk who all the gals are going Madden about, geddit??!? Move over, Poldark, and put your shirt back on 'cos there's a noo kid on the block and he ain't wearing any trousers!?!?!? Ok, so the bodyguard's got complex psychological Post Traumatic Stress Disorder issues?!!? Who cares??!? Is that a gun in your pocket or are you just pleased to see me??!? OK, so you haven't got any trousers or any pockets, but still... Sex stars from this discerning critic!?!?!??

■ WANDERLUST!?!?! Blimey!! It's on BBC1, but it should be on BBC Phwoar!?!? Geddit???! Ok, so it's another programme full of prime-time rumpy pumpy...!??! What's wrong with that, Mr Prude??!? So Lord Reith would be turning in his grave, would he??! I think old Johnny boy would be up for it???!?!? Inform, entertain and fornicate!?!?! *(Surely "educate"? Ed.)*

■ TV WEATHER!??!!! Why has everyone got their clothes on??!? Where's the fun in that??!? Bring on the naked weather forecasters, I say!??!? Particularly Tomasz Schafernaker!??!? I'd like to see *his* warm front after a spell in the isobar and a long shower??!?

Byeee!!

"...I think we're at the wrong Tommy Robinson gig"

TWITTER RALLIES TO DEFENCE OF SERENA WILLIAMS

by Our Social Media Staff **Mimi Too**

A HUGE Twitterstorm erupted yesterday, as fans hit back at criticism of tennis superstar Serena Williams for her controversial behaviour in the final of the US Open tennis tournament.

After Serena's much-publicised disagreement with the umpire, millions of angry supporters protested that Miss Williams had been horribly maligned and discriminated against for her part in the on-court exchanges.

"Why was Serena picked on?" said one typical tweet. "Just for losing her temper, smashing her racket and calling the umpire a thief and liar?"

"It is a basic human right," agreed another, "for any player to behave really badly when they are losing and to threaten the umpire with the loss of his job."

Many others agreed with Ms Williams' claims that she had been the victim of "racist" and "sexist" abuse by the umpire, when all she had been trying to do as "a mother, a woman and a member of the Afro-American community" was to stand up for the right to behave like a spoiled child just because she was being beaten by someone who, unfortunately, was also a woman and also not white, but who didn't see the need to (cont. p94)

Lives of the Saints and Martyrs No.94
St Aung San Suu Kyi of Myanmar

THERE WAS ONCE, in the land that was called Burma, a beautiful and wise young woman, the daughter of the late Aung San, the Father of the Nation. She was called Aung San Suu Kyi (which is a bit like calling your daughter Nigella) and she travelled all the way to the distant city of Oxford to learn how she might one day become the saviour of her people.

On her return, she began to speak out bravely against the evil and power-crazed generals who had enslaved all her countrymen and women, Buddhists and Muslims alike. So popular did she become for speaking out for truth and liberty that the wicked generals locked her away in her own home where the people still looked to her as their chosen leader.

Soon, the story of her courage and virtue spread around the whole world and she was

Suu Kyi take it off again,
Suu Kyi take it off again...
(Old Burmese Nursery Rhyme)

showered with the greatest honours the earth can bestow.

She was hailed as "the New Mandela" and the "heir to Gandhi". She was even awarded the Nobel Prize for Peace, an honour so rare that it was only given to such celebrated makers of peace as Henry Kissinger, Yasser Arafat and the EU.

Eventually, so obvious was the love and respect in which she was held by the people that the generals allowed her to become the first Counsellor of the Nation; equivalent to its prime minister.

And all the world rejoiced and said, "At last Myanmarialand is free under the saintly rule of the Blessed Aung San Suu Kyi".

But then, sadly, an even more terrible darkness returned to the land, as the evil generals – who, in fact, had never gone away – ordered their men to bring about a "final solution" to the problem of all the Muslims.

And so, accordingly, the soldiers went into the land of the Rohingyas, where the Muslims lived, and set about slaughtering them, raping their womenfolk, murdering their infants, burning down their villages and driving them out of the country into the land of Bangladesh.

And all the world looked in horror at these terrible atrocities and said, "Can this really be happening?" And they looked to the saintly Aung San Suu Kyi to intervene. But all the saintly one would say was, "No, it is not happening at all. You are making it all up. Verily, I tell you, it is just fake news."

And in so doing, the scales fell from the eyes of the world, and they realised that this most revered figure in the world was nothing of the kind, but just an empty cardboard figurehead, a hapless puppet of the evil generals and, in fact, a plastic saint .

And when folk understood how they had been duped, they felt extremely foolish and quite cross.

INNOCENT RUSSIAN TOURISTS ENJOY SALISBURY

Let's go and see the cathedral

We've got a bit of time to kill

 **Salisbury** ★★★★★

Review by **Alexander and Ruslan**

As ordinary civilians with no connection whatsoever to the secret service, we had a lovely time in this quaint English rural town. We were so exhausted after one hour's sightseeing that we headed back to our lovely hotel in Bow. The snowy

Places of interest

Mr Skripal's front door

weather was also very difficult for us Russians, because we so rarely see snow in Russia. But we loved Salisbury so much that we went back the next day and had a lot of fun trying to avoid all the CCTV cameras! We had a great time and definitely won't be going there ever again, or indeed anywhere else outside Russia.

PS. *We lost our duty-free perfume somewhere in the area. If found, please don't return.*

The Times, Saturday, September 22, 2018

Did Michael Foot Carry Out The Salisbury Poisonings On Russia's Behalf?

Probably not, as he had been dead for eight years.

TOM WATSON LOSES SEVEN STONE IN DRAMATIC DIET

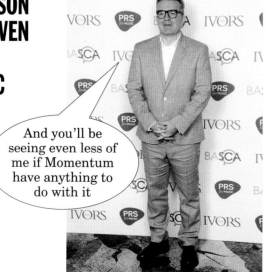

And you'll be seeing even less of me if Momentum have anything to do with it

---

GERRY ADAMS COOK BOOK

"No just desserts, I see..."

BANX

"I want to leave Brexit"

ME AND MY SPOON

THIS WEEK

JACOB REES-MOGG'S NANNY

Do you have a favourite spoon?

Yes, it's this lovely wooden one. I've had it for years.

Do you find your spoon useful in the kitchen?

No. I find it useful for keeping small boys in line. Particularly stubborn ones like young Master Jacob.

So you have no problem with what some people might call spoon-abuse?

Of course not. It's all nonsense. The threat of the spoon encourages honesty, kindness and thoughtfulness in children. Look at Jacob, it hasn't done him any harm.

That's debatable.

How dare you! You take that back, young man, or you will feel the rough end of Nanny's wooden spoon.

I'm not frightened of... ow, that hurt!!

Say sorry to Nanny and sorry to Jacob. Go on.

Ow! Ow! (sobs)

I mean it...

(This interview was sadly then terminated when our reporter was sent to bed without his tea.)

NEXT WEEK: *Peter Bone, Me and My Bone.*

Let's Parlez Franglais!

Numéro 94

La Guerre des Scallops

La scene: un bateau de fishing anglais, vraiment close to la côte de France...

Le Fisher-homme anglais: Oh la la! Voyez tous these scallops que nous avons trouvés au bed de la mer.

Le Fisher-homme français: Oi! Que faîtes-vous avec les scallops français?

Anglais: Je les simmerai dans un frying-pan avec la beurre et le vin blanc. Mmm. Délicieux.

Français: Vous avez stolen notre recipe aussi! Leavez nos scallops alone!

Anglais: Non! Je fillerai mes boots.

Français: Don't vous mean boats?

Anglais: Non – boots! Wellington Boots. That's 'Wellington' comme dans Waterloo. Vous rememberez Trafalgar?

Français: Le Square? Oui, je l'ai visité quand j'étais un touriste teenagé, avant du Hard Rock Café et Madame Tussauds.

Anglais: Cessez de prendre le piss.

(Il mange un scallop dans un gesture provocatif)

Français: Je warn you – takez vos thieving mains off nos scallops!

Anglais: Makez-moi!

Français: Okay, je will!

Anglais: Oh yeah? Vous et qui's Navy!

(Le navy français appears sur l'horizon)

Anglais: Oh merde!

Français: Allez back to les waters anglais!

Anglais: Non, ils sont trop full of plastique. Et un long distance swimmer!

(Le fisher-homme français then jette un stone)

Français: Prennez ça, rosbif!

Anglais: Ouch, ce n'est pas cricket.

Français: Non – c'est la guerre.

Anglais: Dans that case, nous launcherons notre weapon secrete!

(Un object vraiment étrange appears sur le pont du bateau anglais)

Français: Sacré blue! Qu'est-ce que that?! C'est un monstre. Un slippery, oily poisson from le deep.

Anglais: Non – c'est Michael Gove, le Secrétaire d' Etat pour l'Agriculture, les Fisheries et la Nourriture.

Français: AFN? Vous parlez le gibberish.

Mr Gove: Non, c'est moi qui parle le gibberish. Vive le Brexit! Le plain sailing! Les skies bleus! Les waters tranquilles! Pas de storm sur l'horizon! Etc, etc.

(Le bateau anglais sinks)

© *The late nautical kilometres Kington.*

Oi! Zat is our scallop!

LONG-DISTANCE SWIMMER ARRIVES IN DOVER

No papers? I'm afraid you're going to have to go back to where you came from

---

HURRICANE FLORENCE — TRUMP TAKES CONTROL

by Our Weather Staff **Gail Force**

AS THE latest powerful tropical storm, Hurricane Florence, sweeps across the Eastern seaboard, threatening to leave a trail of devastation and destruction in its wake, President Trump has personally taken control of the situation.

The president tweeted from his bedroom at 3am: "I have never met Hurricane Florence. I never slept with her. Unless she is that friend of Stormy Daniels."

Mr Trump took some time to consider his position and at 3.01 qualified his earlier tweet with: "Oh hang on, it's all coming back to me. Hurricane Florence signed a non-disclosure agreement and has nothing further to say on the matter. I got my lawyer to deal with it all. But I did not pay her money."

He continued, at 3.02: "Okay, so I did pay her money, but it wasn't from campaign funds, it was from my own personal bank account," before adding at 3.03, "Alright, it was from campaign funds, but in no way was it a huge donation from the Russians. Call off this witch hunt now."

At 3.05, while America slept on, unaware of the drama unfolding in the president's head, Mr Trump tried some damage limitation, tweeting: "Okay, it may have been Russian money, but I didn't know about it, which makes it fake news. #failingNewYorkTimes."

At 3.06 he tweeted: "Why have the cartoons been taken off to show me some boring wind storm? #failingCartoonNetwork."

By 3.10, the crisis appeared to be over, as Trump demanded the extradition of Speedy Gonzalez on charges of rape, murder and drug peddling.

HOW'S MY DRAINING?

K.J.Lamb

The Eye's Controversial New Columnist

The columnist who is very glad Marmite is leaving for the Netherlands, and hopes mashed broccoli will join it

This week I am very angry about Jo Swinson bringing her baby into the Commons chamber. This makes a mockery of our system of democracy when an unqualified baby can get onto those fabled green benches and just gurgle a bit, when there are other far more qualified babies available; ones able to make stirring speeches in favour of capital punishment, cutting benefits and going to war with France. Why was this baby allowed access when so many other babies try and fail to get into the Commons? When I stood as leader of Youkip, a party specifically created to advocate for more naps in the afternoon, I was defeated in 12 by-elections. If the rules have changed so that I can get into the Commons just by waking up in the afternoon and being a bit grouchy then I should have been told that this was the case and *(cont. p94)*

Revealed: the two letters Boris wrote to his wife

by Our Entire Staff B.R. EXIT

This magazine can exclusively reveal that Boris Johnson, the former Foreign Secretary, actually composed two very different letters to his wife Marina before the world learned of the break-up of their 25-year-long marriage.

Whilst everyone assumed that Boris's decision had been long considered and was based on a carefully worked-out plan to leave, the second letter tells a very different story.

In the first letter, hitherto unseen by the public, Johnson makes the case for remaining in the marriage, in the hope that he will get away with his latest infidelity and that his wife will not throw him out.

The letters show that Johnson was completely in two minds as to whether to leave or remain, and on the biggest issue to confront his marriage in 45 years, he hadn't a clue which way to play it.

Those letters, recovered from the Johnson household's recycling bins, in full

The REMAIN Letter

My dearest Marina,

After long and careful consideration, I have decided that it would be in the best interests of everyone concerned that we remain together as we have done through all these years.

Tempting though it may be for us to imagine that a divorce would in some way lead to the chance of starting a new independent life and new opportunities for a bright and sunlit future elsewhere, I have decided that it would be much more responsible for us to stay together and try to make our marriage work.

I now realise that the alternative is quite unthinkable, and could only lead to needless and bitter acrimony, not to mention a political and economic disaster for myself.

I hope I have made my position entirely clear.

Yours,

Boris *(former Foreign Secretary and Mayor of London, and future Conservative Prime Minister of the United Kingdom)*

The LEAVE Letter

Dear Marina,

After long and serious consideration, I have decided that it is in the interests of everyone concerned that I should make a complete and clean exit from our marriage as soon as possible.

Only on this basis can we look forward to enjoying the sunlit uplands of a bright new future, in which I will be free to find exciting new partners all over the world.

I am sure we will come to a very good deal that can be amicably negotiated, even though you obviously want to see the back of me and will be asking quite unreasonably for a divorce settlement of £39 billion, which is the equivalent of at least three of my columns for the Daily Telegraph.

Yours,

Boris *(former Foreign Secretary, Mayor of London and Husband)*

We can either move to bigger offices or stop bringing in donuts.

Church of England revealed to be major investor in Hell

by Our Religious Staff
St Matthew Parris

The C of E was deeply embarrassed last night when it was discovered to be a major shareholder in Eternal Damnation plc, run by its chief executive, Jeff Bezelzibos, known as the underworld's richest man.

There have been disturbing stories about Hell, including the mistreatment of personnel who endure zero hours contracts with no toilet breaks and are prodded with tridents by horned devils whilst they burn in an everlasting fire.

The Archbishop of Canterbury attempted to play down the Church's involvement, saying, "It is only by being part of such enterprises that we can effect change from the inside.

"This could make me look very silly"

It is not hypocritical to make sensible investments in Hell.

"Didn't Our Lord himself say it is easier for a camel to pass through the eye of a needle than for an Amazon package to get through your letterbox?"

He then added, "Let us pay. Or, rather, in Mr Bezelzibos' case, let us *not* pay."

DEPT. FOR EXCITING THE EU

Jeremy Corbyn WRITES

HELLO! It's me again. Well, it seems the hated mainstream media are out again, spreading rumours that John McDonnell is going to try to challenge me for the leadership of the Labour Party.

Can I remind you that John is a loyal party man, an ideological comrade and a brother in socialism? Which means the rumours may well be true.

Now, I'm not keen on this notion of challenging for the leadership. Granted, some of the older Momentum members might remember when I advocated a vote every year for party leader, but let's not forget I said that when Tony Blair was leader, not me! I don't believe that anymore. So that's certainly one in the eye for my critics who say I never changed my position on anything!

No, my position on who runs Labour is much the same as my position on Brexit. We had a vote; we got a result I liked and so that is the settled will of the people for ever and ever and ever, no matter how calamitous it gets!

However, just in case, I've got Seumas Milne to work up a dossier to use against Mr McDonnell. Apparently, he's had a very long history of cosying up to terrorists across the globe AND he's got a track record of hostility against our armed forces and our police. It seems that whenever there's a conflict we're involved in, he always takes the side that isn't British!

We don't want someone like THAT in charge of one of our great national parties, do we?

Cheerio!

'I WILL ONLY TALK TO ANYONE'
Meghan's Dad gives exclusive interview

by Our Royal Staff
Ivor Bigmouth

THE troubled relationship between Mr Thomas Markle, the estranged father of the Duchess of Sussex, and the British press reached a new low yesterday.

Said Mr Markle, "I've been ringing every day and no one wants to talk to me."

He continued, "I thought we had a great relationship. They seemed to love me and care deeply about my life, but it seems now that the press is embarrassed to have any contact with me. It's like they don't want to know."

Mr Markle then confessed to various answering machines in Fleet Street, "I'm heartbroken. The press are just like the Scientologists. They are a sinister cult intent on making money out of innocent people. Where's that cheque you promised?"

A press spokesman, however, refused to comment. "This is a private matter between Mr Markle and ourselves. It would be wrong for us to suggest that Mr Markle has run out of decent stories and we are about to drop him for ever."

CAR ACCIDENTALLY DRIVEN ONTO RAILWAY LINE

Get it off the track before a train comes...

...that gives us at least three days

---

10 Years On From The Financial Crisis, We List The Changes That Have Made The World's Banks Safe And Stable

1.

2.

3.

4.

5.

6.

7.

8.

9. Er…

10. That's it.

Autumn Blockbusters
Groundhog May

■ Doomed to repeat an unending daily routine, Theresa May wakes up every day to face exactly the same problems, as the radio plays "I've Got EU, Babe".

Depressed by the grim forecasts of Punxsutawney Phil Hammond, who predicts an endless winter, Theresa tries every day to think of a new way to escape from this repetitive cycle of misery. She tries to learn French, she befriends a drunk (in a delightful cameo by Jean-Claude Juncker), she even drives off a cliff, but nothing works, it's always the same story again.

The real horror comes when she wakes up to find it is no longer Groundhog May and tomorrow is March 29th 2019.

EYE RATING: Not funny at all.

Nursery Times

·········· Friday, Once-upon-a-time ··········

OBESITY CRISIS ROCKS NURSERYLAND

by Our Obesity Staff **Plumpty Dumpty**

MEDICAL authorities in Nurseryland (all the king's horses and all the king's men) today warned that Nurseryland was now the fattest imaginary country in the world.

Said Doctor Foster, on his way to a conference in Gloucester, "It's out of control, everywhere I go I see evidence of chronic obesity."

The cases have begun to stretch the NHS (Nurseryland Health Service) to its limit. One girl, Alice, once small enough to go down a rabbit hole, complained, "It's not my fault, I saw a sign saying 'Eat Me' on all the food in the fridge, so I did, and I'm now the size of a house, literally."

Elsewhere, the mystery of what happened to Little Bo Peep's missing sheep was solved by the appearance of Big Bo Peep, licking her lips. "Okay, so I ate them, so what? Stop fat shaming me!"

Doctor Foster claims that the crisis cuts across all classes, "It's not just working-class shepherdesses eating junk sheep, princesses are also victims. There's one I know who wouldn't eat her greens, leaving her pea untouched, and consuming a pile of mattresses instead.

"And don't get me started on Goldilocks, she's beginning the day with enough porridge to feed three bears – no wonder she broke the chair! As for Jack Spratt, well, such is the power of food advertising, he now eats only fat."

The ramifications of the crisis are far reaching. A homeless witch complained that two children had eaten her entire gingerbread house and, when she tried to shove them in the oven, they were too fat.

Said Doctor Foster, "People have got to start counting their calories, or at least how many blackbirds they bake in a pie. Four and twenty is more than enough for the average adult! Now, someone help me out of this puddle – my middle is so fat, I'm stuck in it."

On other pages

● Big surprise as Teddy Bears' picnic cancelled in health drive **3** ● Knave of Hearts forbidden to eat tarts **24** ● Newspapers unhealthily full of obesity stories **728**

Exclusive to all newspapers

WHO IS THE MYSTERY BLOND WHO IS THE LOVE OF BORIS'S LIFE?

FLIRTY, funny, party-loving, vivacious, and politically ambitious, we can at last reveal the identity of the blond bombshell who has won Boris's heart.

It's none other than Boris Johnson. The ex-foreign secretary fell in love with himself many years ago and is willing to risk everything and anything to make himself happy.

Said one friend of Boris, "When Boris caught a glimpse of himself in the mirror, it was love at first sight. He's been besotted ever since, and utterly in thrall to his own charm. Nothing will stand in the way of his overwhelming passion for himself. Boris is like a Romeo to his Romeo."

Said Boris to himself at a recent political ball, "You're the one, Boris. You complete me. You had me at 'Cripes'."

A SIDEWAYS LOOK...

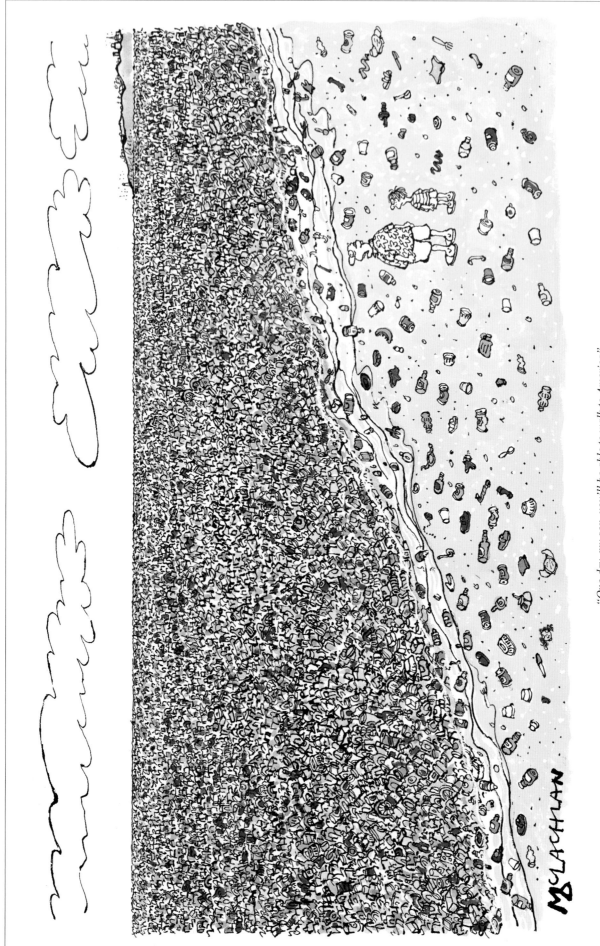

"One day, my son, you'll be able to walk to America"